ENGAGE
EVERY PARENT!

Encouraging Families to **SIGN ON, SHOW UP,**
and **MAKE A DIFFERENCE**

NANCY TELLETT-ROYCE and **SUSAN WOOTTEN**

SEARCH
INSTITUTE
PRESS

Engage Every Parent! Encouraging Families to Sign On, Show Up, and Make a Difference

Nancy Tellett-Royce and Susan Wootten

The following are registered trademarks of Search Institute: Search Institute®, Developmental Assets®, and

Search Institute Press, Minneapolis, MN
Copyright © 2008 by Search Institute

At the time of publication, all facts and figures cited herein are the most current available; all telephone numbers, addresses, and Web site URLs are accurate and active; all publications, organizations, Web sites, and other resources exist as described in this book; and all efforts have been made to verify them. The authors and Search Institute make no warranty or guarantee concerning the information and materials given out by organizations or content found at Web sites that are cited herein, and we are not responsible for any changes that occur after this book's publication. If you find an error or believe that a resource listed herein is not as described, please contact Client Services at Search Institute.

10 9 8 7 6 5 4 3 2 1
Printed on acid-free paper in the United States of America.

Search Institute

615 First Avenue Northeast, Suite 125
Minneapolis, MN 55413
www.search-institute.org
612-376-8955 • 800-888-7828

ISBN-13: 978-1-57482-194-9

Credits

Editors: Alison Dotson, Susan Wootten
Copy Editor: Jill Lafferty
Book Design: Percolator
Production Supervisor: Mary Ellen Buscher

Library of Congress Cataloging-in-Publication Data

Tellett-Royce, Nancy.
    Engage every parent! : encouraging families to sign on, show up, and make a difference / Nancy Tellett-Royce and Susan Wootten.
      p. cm.
    Includes bibliographical references and index.
    ISBN 978-1-57482-194-9 (pbk. : alk. paper)
    1. Education—Parent participation. 2. Parent and child. 3. Volunteer workers in education. I. Wootten, Susan. II. Title.
    LB1048.5.T45 2008
    371.19′2—dc22

                        2008017123

About Search Institute Press

Search Institute Press is a division of Search Institute, a nonprofit organization that offers leadership, knowledge, and resources to promote positive youth development. Our mission at Search Institute Press is to provide practical and hope-filled resources to help create a world in which all young people thrive. Our products are embedded in research, and the 40 Developmental Assets—qualities, experiences, and relationships youth need to succeed—are a central focus of our resources. Our logo, the SIP flower, is a symbol of the thriving and healthy growth young people experience when they have an abundance of assets in their lives.

CONTENTS

Introduction

I remember being called to the principal's office in first grade. Although the occasion was a positive one, I was nervous. However, Mr. Siegel put me at ease with his generous smile. He asked me to deliver a manila envelope to my father, who was chair of the PTA that year. I still recall how happy I was to be entrusted with this important task, and how proud I was of my dad.

Later, when my own children entered preschool, there was no doubt in my mind that I, too, would become involved in their education. I knew it mattered, and I looked forward to this part of parenting. During the many years my children were growing up, I eventually met many parents who were able to become involved in their child's school and after-school activities, as well as some parents who faced substantial barriers that made their engagement difficult. This book will help you identify and work to remove those barriers, and take action to reach as many parents as possible, with the goal being to *engage every parent.*

Young people can thrive when teachers, coaches, youth leaders, and program providers communicate effectively with parents and establish worthwhile relationships. If you work with children and adolescents, you have tremendous influence over the experiences and opportunities that help young people grow into healthy, responsible, and caring adults. At Search Institute, we call these experiences and opportunities Developmental Assets. (See page 77 for a list of the 40 Developmental Assets for Adolescents.) After conducting extensive research, the institute created a framework of 40 assets and identified them as integral to the healthy development of children and adolescents. Search Institute has found that the greater the number of assets young people have, the more likely they'll be successful as adults. (For more information about the Developmental Assets and for links to multiple translations of the asset lists for all ages, see www.search-institute.org/assets.) When you intentionally partner with parents, you have even richer opportunities to contribute to the lives of the youth you serve.

You know that parent engagement matters. Perhaps you want to encourage parents to participate more fully in their children's education, whether it's through home-based actions such as helping kids recognize patterns, teaching them letters and numbers, signing permission slips, reviewing report cards, or consistently checking homework assignments. Or maybe you'd like to encourage parents to ensure that kids come to activities and lessons on time, rested, and fed, or

SIX TYPES OF PARENT INVOLVEMENT

The national Parent Teacher Association (PTA) has developed standards for parent/family partnerships based upon six types of parent involvement identified by Joyce L. Epstein, Ph.D., of the Center on School, Family, and Community Partnerships at Johns Hopkins University.

The PTA's parent involvement standards, based on Epstein's framework, are as follows[i]:

Standard 1: Welcoming all families into the school community—Families are active participants in the life of the school, and feel welcomed, valued, and connected to each other, to school staff, and to what students are learning and doing in class.

Standard 2: Communicating effectively—Families and school staff engage in regular, two-way, and meaningful communication about student learning.

Standard 3: Supporting student success—Families and school staff continuously collaborate to support students' learning and healthy development both at home and at school, and have regular opportunities to strengthen their knowledge and skills to do so effectively.

Standard 4: Speaking up for every child—Families are empowered to be advocates for their own and other children, to ensure that students are treated fairly and have access to learning opportunities that will support their success.

Standard 5: Sharing power—Families and school staff are equal partners in decisions that affect children and families and together inform, influence, and create policies, practices, and programs.

Standard 6: Collaborating with community—Families and school staff collaborate with community members to connect students, families, and staff to expanded learning opportunities, community services, and civic participation.

---

[i] National Standards for Family-School Partnerships, *What Parents, Schools, and Communities Can Do Together to Support Student Success*, PTA, 2007.

attend their school conferences, sports games, school events, and club activities. And then there is the more ambitious goal of empowering parents to take on substantial leadership commitments, such as fundraising for community-based or school-run programs, hosting and leading meetings, becoming involved in decision-making groups, or volunteering on a regular basis in after-school, faith-based, or school settings. Whatever form your goals take for active parent involvement in their children's lives, you'll find support and resources in this book to help you accomplish your aims.

How to Use This Book

This book is for you, whether you're a new or seasoned teacher, coach, parent outreach coordinator, faith community leader, community organization leader, after-school activity coordinator, or youth program provider. You'll find numerous ideas to effectively engage and inspire busy parents and caregivers in your work. Each chapter includes ready-to-use handouts, timesaving tips, strategies to empower parents and guardians, and pertinent stories and suggestions to give you fresh motivation for your parent engagement work. This book takes the following form:

Chapter 1—Identifying Your Goals for Parent Engagement offers several suggestions for goals you can set to encourage parent engagement, and ideas for reaching those goals.

Chapter 2—Communicating Effectively with Parents will help you address each stage of your relationship with parents, from your initial meeting to dealing with problems regarding their child. This chapter describes the many forms of communication you can use with parents and how to best implement them.

Chapter 3—Reaching Out to Build Positive Relationships with All Parents offers tips on becoming acquainted with parents across a variety of settings and from a multitude of backgrounds. This chapter discusses how to maintain ongoing, open relationships with parents and share relevant information about their children in a positive way.

Chapter 4—Meeting Parents One-on-One suggests ways you can navigate meetings with parents in academic and nonacademic settings, and offers a new spin on what meetings should achieve for kids, parents, and you.

Chapter 5—Icebreakers for Group Gatherings contains ideas for group activities that will help parents get to know each other and show them how fun and beneficial parent involvement can be.

Chapter 6—Recruiting and Managing Parent Volunteers gives tips on how best to meet children's needs by making effective use of parent volunteers' time. Included are ways you can maintain a positive and productive relationship with parent volunteers.

Chapter 7—Empowering Parents to Be Successful Leaders extends parent involvement beyond the basics to include advocacy, fundraising, decision making, and community building.

Chapter 8—Appreciating and Celebrating Parent Involvement suggests a variety of ways to thank parents for partnering with you to help their children experience success.

A Note about Language

For the purposes of this book, we use the word *parent* to refer to the primary caregivers who are connected to and support the children and youth in your classes, in your programs, and on your teams. While the use of *parent* in the book's title and text is used for ease of reading, we recognize that the children and youth you work with may be raised in homes where, instead of or in addition to a biological parent, their primary caregiver is a grandparent or other extended family member, foster parent, stepparent, or caring guardian.

What Is an "Engaged Parent"?

What does it mean to be an engaged parent? To begin, let's look at the conditions that point to parents' involvement in their children's lives. You know how much easier your job is when youth show up on time, have been fed, and are energized, well rested, and prepared. These conditions occur when parents make sure children eat on a regular schedule, make a concerted effort to complete homework, and follow family rules for curfews and bedtime.

This book offers strategies to engage and work with all parents, regardless of their situation. Some parents struggle with the basic tasks of parenting, while others are able to go beyond the demands of parenting at home to be physically present for their children at school and in extracurricular activities. The reasons for these differences are complex. Single parents who work two or even three jobs simply won't be as physically available as parents in some dual-income families, who may have more flexible work schedules and resources. Some stay-at-home parents whose children are enrolled in school full-time may be more readily available—but only if they also have transportation, speak and understand English, and feel comfortable stepping into an unfamiliar environment.

Your expectations for each parent's level of involvement with their children's academic and social worlds will necessarily differ. It is important not to judge parents who aren't involved with their children in ways that you can easily observe, or in ways that you would like them to be. It's also important not to compare relative levels of parent involvement within families. Each family deals with its own set of unique personal circumstances.

Identifying Your Goals
for Parent Engagement

If you've ever asked a group of teachers, coaches, clergy, and youth leaders about their experiences with parents, you've probably received a great variety of responses:

- "The same parents always volunteer for everything."

- "My team parent coordinator is key to our success. I don't know what I'd do without her."

- "I asked for Parent Night volunteers, but only one parent signed up."

- "I sent home volunteer sign-up sheets with the kids, and almost every parent sent one back."

- "While we only have two concerts a year, some parents never seem to make it."

- "Our program relies on parents to share transportation to 'away' games, and I'm happy to say the parents don't let me down."

- "Four parents said they would chaperone the field trip, but only one came. It was a nightmare!"

All forms of parent engagement, no matter how small they may seem, are beneficial for your students or program participants. Almost every school, congregation, sports association, or youth program has parent volunteers who know how to "make a difference." Other parents need a little encouragement, reassurance, and information about what they'll be expected to do in order to tip the balance between staying home and getting involved.

While it's true that some parents rarely show up and don't respond to sign-up sheets sent home in backpacks or posted on bulletin boards, there are ways to draw them in to attend school or program functions

WHAT ARE THE BENEFITS OF PARENT ENGAGEMENT...

For Schools?

- Teacher morale improves.
- Parents give teachers higher ratings.
- Families offer teachers and students more support.
- Students reach a higher level of academic achievement.
- Community perceptions of the school improve.

For Parents?

- Parents develop more confidence in the school.
- The teachers they work with have higher opinions of them as parents and higher expectations of their children.
- Parents develop more confidence not only about helping their children learn at home, but also about themselves as parents.

For Students?

- Students achieve higher grades and test scores.
- Attendance improves and more homework is completed.
- Fewer students are placed in special education.
- Students exhibit more positive attitudes and behavior.
- Graduation rates increase.
- Enrollment in postsecondary education increases.

Henderson, A. T., and Berla, N., eds., *A New Generation of Evidence: The Family Is Critical to Student Achievement*, (Washington, D.C.: Center for Law and Education, 1994).

and volunteer on-site. Many schools and programs that have successfully recruited volunteers say the first step is to *identify the specific goals* for parent engagement, and act on effective strategies that will help meet those goals.

What Do You Need from Parents?

Public Agenda, a national nonprofit organization, surveyed 1,220 parents of children in public schools and 1,000 public school teachers about parental involvement. Among the findings was this point of agreement:

> *Both parents and teachers believe that the most fundamental and indispensable job for parents is raising well-behaved children who want to learn. For both groups, the same basic lessons—respect, effort, self-control—emerge again and again as the essentials that every child must master before academic learning can even begin.*[1]

This information doesn't apply only to the classroom—these social skills are necessary for success in all areas of life, including team sports, musical groups, and youth groups. It is best if both you and each child's parents help the child build these skills with an eye to healthy interaction within a peer group, whether this interaction occurs in a classroom, on a team, or in a program. (See handouts "Goal Setting: What Do You Need from Parents and Families?" on page 79 and "Getting Organized for the School Year" on page 80.)

Goal: Clear, Two-Way Communication

When you think about the communication skills you work on with young people, it's likely that you spend time at the beginning of the program year clearly naming the rules that will guide how they should communicate with you and their peers. Being intentional about laying the ground rules for interaction helps you keep misunderstandings to a minimum and encourages direct, respectful, and complete communication of information.

Many communication problems involving parents and schools or youth programs are rooted in the first contacts that teachers or program providers initiate to alert parents to their children's academic or social issues. When a child or teen is having a hard time showing respect, demonstrating effort, or exhibiting self-control, the teacher, coach, or other program leader often initiates a conversation with the young person's parent. While you won't be setting communication "rules" for parents at the beginning of your academic or program year, you *can* model good communication skills by sharing complete, concise information with them and letting them know what forms of communication they can expect from you (for example, through newsletters, phone calls, e-mails, and Web postings).

Invite parents to communicate with you, and make it easy for them by providing your contact information in writing. Offer your phone number and e-mail address on paper that can be posted on the refrigerator or included in a three-ring binder. List phone numbers you feel comfortable sharing, whether that means your work number, cell phone number, or your home number as well, and your e-mail address and times or days when you are most likely to be available.

Be sure to name the reasons you want to keep open lines of communication with parents. Tell parents in direct terms how clear, complete communication between them and you will have a positive influence on their child's progress. For example, when you both have a common understanding of a concern, you can work together to come up with a plan that suits everyone. It's reasonable to let parents know you'll respond to their calls or e-mails within 48 hours. Prompt communication on your part also means parents can expect to receive any important last-minute changes from you that might affect their schedules, transportation arrangements, and expectations for the program. And clear, appropriate oral and written communications will help establish the conditions necessary for building genuine and lasting relationships based upon your mutual interest—the personal growth and success of the kids in your program.

Goal: Solving the Parent-Child-Homework Equation

The amount of homework students receive has increased dramatically in the past decade as schools increase the rigor of their academic programs to address more stringent test performance benchmarks, higher achievement expectations, and the demands of a 21st-century workplace. Forming a family/school partnership that focuses on homework completion may be one of the most critical goals you have for parent engagement. (See handout "Touch Base!" on page 81.)

Parents name fights with their children over homework as one of the areas they like least about parenting. And it's no wonder. Teachers express considerable frustration when students come to school unprepared. It is likely that there is a direct connection between the two situations. Because there have been so many changes in the amount and type of homework expected of students in recent years, it will be critical to explain to parents why you assign the homework you do, and what your expectations are for parents in helping their children complete assignments. Parents need to know how and why expectations for homework have changed, and why it is important to have parents "buy in" to the process. Their homework support roles will vary, depending on a child's grade level and individual characteristics.

In some cases, parents must work late shifts or multiple jobs to support their families. Children may often be enrolled in after-school activities or programs, or must care for younger siblings and help prepare meals when they return home. It is all too easy for homework time to be squeezed out of a child's day if time is not intentionally set aside for it. In addition, parents may not think they know enough about a particular subject to feel competent when it comes to helping with homework. Parents may not speak English as their first language, making it very difficult for them to assist their children when they become "stuck" with a problem or need help with a reading passage. And at any time, a family that has been doing well may suddenly suffer a major family illness, job loss, or a relationship separation that pulls everyone's attention away from children's daily activities, including their homework.

Finally, a less-obvious barrier to homework completion can arise when parents become overinvolved in children's homework assignments. Parents who plan, direct, and complete their children's assignments for them penalize their children without realizing the long-term consequences of their actions. If you notice that a student has done a wonderful job on homework but rarely knows the answers in class or fares poorly on tests, her parent may be too hands-on with homework.

All children, regardless of ability, talent, interest, and circumstances, need time to practice new skills and learn from their mistakes, an opportunity that homework offers them in the first place. In addition, completing homework allows children to gain a more complete understanding of the subject and the motivation to pursue knowledge for its own sake. If you notice that a student consistently fails to complete assigned homework, be sure to notify parents promptly so you can work together to find a solution. Don't wait for multiple missed assignments to bring this situation to a parent's attention. (See pages 82 and 83 for more information on homework solutions.)

Goal: Volunteers

Parent volunteers are more commonly found in elementary schools than in middle or high schools. In fact, parents of older children often mention they are told by school staff that "your child won't want you around during the school day" now that they are in middle school. While children begin to express an appropriate and growing need for autonomy as they enter the middle school years, it is important to find ways to continue bringing caring adults into the lives of young people as they move through the upper grades. Parent volunteers are a prime source for these relationships. Once the basics of your plan to recruit volunteers are in place, you can begin thinking about how parent volunteers can best help you meet the needs of your classroom or program.

What tasks do you have for parent volunteers to take on? Some teachers, coaches, and program leaders prefer not to have parents observe them in action, while others welcome the audience. Regardless, both types of teachers and program leaders can use the support and assistance of parents willing to take direction and act as supporting cast members. Are you willing to assign tasks that might not be done *exactly* the way you would perform them? Think about the range of volunteer assignments you could assign, and be flexible about how parents might actually carry them out. Remember, your goal is to empower parents to join with you in creating conditions that lead to their children's successes.

If you talk to peers to get their parent involvement ideas or brainstorm your own ways to engage parents, you'll probably generate a long list. Consider whether you'll have volunteer outreach and management help from a parent coordinator, school staff member, or district employee to accomplish your wish list. This will help you determine a reasonable set of high-priority tasks that parents could perform.

Perhaps your top priorities as a classroom teacher include boosting reading and math test scores. If you're a drama coach, your primary need may be for someone to manage costumes or props so that you have more time to work with your young actors and actresses. Or perhaps you've set goals for individual youth that can best be reached by spending concentrated one-on-one tutoring time with them. Whether a parent volunteer works with that young person individually or with the larger group while you offer the individual assistance, your volunteer's help can allow you to meet your goal.

Additionally, parent volunteers can provide youth with cultural awareness opportunities, positive male and female role models, and various types of enrichment activities. Getting to know parents' special talents, skills, and interests will allow you to uncover additional ideas that fit your program goals. One way to do this is to simply ask parents to send you an e-mail or give you a call to express their interests or availability. More formally, you can send parents a brief skill and talent survey and ask open-ended questions that they can fill in with their particular areas of interest. (See handout "Share Your Parenting Skills, Hobbies, and Interests!" on page 84.)

Goal: Positive Outcomes for Young People

After you identify intended parent involvement outcomes for your program, review your original goals to see if they remain relevant. Most likely you're trying to engage parents not only because education research says you should, but also because you expect certain positive results. Some of your goals for parent involvement may relate directly to intended outcomes in the parent-child relationship. Your other goals and hoped-for outcomes may relate to the progress of the entire class, school, team, or youth program, or to your own sense of well-being. Reprioritize any goals that won't help you reach your outcomes. Add other goals where you identify gaps.

For example, if the outcome you are working toward is to have a student consistently finish and turn in his homework, then include as one of your goals engaging his parents in the homework process. If, as a coach, your desired outcome is a positive team attitude, identify and make parent attendance and upbeat cheering at sports events your goals. If you see these outcomes occur, you'll know your parent engagement efforts are paying off.

What Do Parents Need from You?

The majority of parents want their children to experience success and perform well in school and extracurricular activities. They want their children to be loved, appreciated, and recognized for the great individuals they are. Most parents realize this individual recognition is tougher for an adult to offer in a group of 30 than in a family of four. Nevertheless, they pin their hopes on caring adults who will treat their children with fairness, communicate clearly with them, ensure their children's safety, and make learning an engaging experience—both inside and outside the classroom.

Parents also have other hopes: that their children are giving them the full story when they say everything is going fine; that when they say they have no homework assignments, that really is the case; that the songs for their next piano lesson have been mastered; or that their youth group has never been better. But beyond these hopes, parents count on teachers, program leaders, and coaches to fill in the inevitable communication gaps and make sure all is *really* going well.

Parents' desire to be helpful and supportive of their children is tempered by many other demands on their time. If they are to become engaged, they need to have the following information from you:

- The specific tasks and what they involve.

- The estimated time commitment for the tasks.

- Positive feedback from you.

Parents' motivations for volunteering range from the most altruistic (wanting to help *all* children learn and benefit from school, sports participation, service opportunities, or faith exploration) to closer-to-home (desiring a closer relationship with their child's teacher or observing how much individual attention their child is receiving). You can address much of what parents want by communicating to them that their participation not only strengthens their own child's commitment to school, sports, music, or other program areas, but it also *supports the commitment of other children.* In the same way you discuss your expectations with young people in your classroom, program, or team at the beginning of the year, you can share with parents your hopes and expectations for their own involvement at home, at school, and in extracurricular activities.

Finally, remember that the primary reason for engaging parents is that it has a positive impact on young people's lives. Of course, some youth will feel conflicted over their parents' involvement in their activities. When children are young, they're generally thrilled to have their parent visit the class, lead their Brownie troop, or coach their Little League team. As they grow older, and particularly as they reach the preteen and teenage years, they are less likely to express enthusiasm about having their parents directly involved in their activities. But that doesn't mean there are no good ways to engage parents. It does mean you'll need to look at the types of parent involvement that will work best for all concerned.

When youth are prepared and excited to learn, practice, or perform, your job becomes easier and more rewarding. Instead of managing unruly or uninterested kids, you will be able to focus on the task at hand—teaching, coaching, and guiding young people!

REALITY CHECK

Although the purpose of this book is to equip you with the tools and strategies you need to engage parents, the truth is that there are some parents who will never be engaged in their child's life outside the home. Some parents may be physically or mentally ill, coping with substance abuse, or so strapped for money that they need to work as often as they can. While this is unfortunate, the end goal of engaging parents is educated and well-rounded youth, so employing the help of other parents and caring adults can benefit young people. This doesn't mean you have to give up on uninvolved parents; in fact, building and maintaining a relationship with them now may ensure that they will be more likely to get involved in the future.

Reaching Every Parent—In the Classroom

You're probably accustomed to working with many different kinds of learners and their various levels of comprehension, enthusiasm, and attentiveness. Just as your students have unique personalities and situations, so do their parents. How can you engage all parents, not just those who eagerly volunteer their time before you even have a chance to ask for help?

Some parents have the ability to go above and beyond an expected level of involvement in their children's activities and education, assisting not only their own children, but acting in the interests of all students at the school. Others have so little free time that they barely have time to talk to their child, let alone help with homework, attend games or concerts, or participate in parent-teacher conferences. It's understandable to feel frustrated and saddened by the situation these students face, but it's important to take into account a family's individual needs and circumstances.

When a student rarely finishes the homework you assign, it's reasonable to talk to the student and to the student's parents. You may discover the reason the student is doing poorly in school is more complicated than you might imagine or assume. Perhaps the student lives with an ill, single parent, and so the student must spend his evenings assuming household responsibilities—cleaning, shopping for groceries, making dinner, or babysitting younger siblings. The challenge is to find innovative ways to make school an enjoyable and meaningful experience for this student.

Unfortunately, there are some situations in which you will never be able to engage a student's parent to the point that they will be available to volunteer inside or outside the classroom or help with homework. When you realize this, you'll need to go beyond the parent's physical presence and come up with solutions that will ensure your student's academic success.

While you never want to give up trying to engage a parent's attention and focus on her child, in the meantime that child needs to establish a homework routine that works and perhaps get extra academic help or tutoring. This is where available parent volunteers come in. Although a parent may volunteer his time to help his own child, it is often the students who do not have such engaged parents who need the most help and attention in the classroom—and beyond.

> " *Many parents—especially low-income parents or those who lack a college degree—feel intimidated in school settings, and feel that what they think doesn't count very much.* "
>
> Recruiting New Teachers, Inc., *Connect for Success: Building a Teacher, Parent, Teen Alliance* (Belmont, Mass.: RNC, Inc, 2001), 20.

Reaching Every Parent—On the Field, after School, and in the Pews

If you work with students after school as an athletic coach, play director, program director, or youth pastor, you may find that some young people face obstacles in meeting the time commitments necessary for the whole group's success.

The first step to solving these problems is to sit down and have a private conversation with the individual. But don't stop there. It's possible that parents don't know their child hasn't been attending regularly or on time, and they might have insights to help you understand the child's poor attendance record. Work with parents to identify barriers to full participation and come up with clever solutions.

If you discover that parents are uncomfortable with their child's participation, find out why. There could be any number of reasons, and you may be able to convince parents of the importance of their child's involvement in extracurricular activities. Perhaps the team sport or program is cost-prohibitive, or the parents are originally from a culture that doesn't understand or support the activity. Perhaps parents need their child at home in the evening to help with chores or younger siblings, care for an ailing relative, or work a part-time job to make ends meet.

What can you do? Your school or organization may have financial aid for participants who can't afford the equipment, clothes, or program fees. If you don't, consider implementing a scholastic program. You can share with parents the many benefits their child will experience by being a member of your club, team, or group. Invite them to attend a practice or rehearsal so they can see what it's all about. Try to think creatively—is it possible for the young person to rearrange her work schedule to better accommodate extracurricular activities? Are there on-site tasks or jobs you can pay the teenager to take on that will allow her to participate in practice, rehearsal, or after-school activities? You may wonder how these actions help engage parents. The answer is that some parents are truly unable to attend events, provide transportation, or afford certain programs. These are tough hurdles to overcome, so instead of focusing attention on the parents' limitations or giving up on them entirely, fill in the gaps whenever possible.

You can take other actions to help participants who often show up late—or not at all. Chances are, they do care about the program or extracurricular activity and wish they had more control over their circumstances. Perhaps a young person can't get a ride home from practice or rehearsal, so she takes the school bus home instead of

One mom solved our transportation crisis. Because her daughter has relatively few friends outside our program for adolescent girls, she placed a high value on her daughter's participation and wanted to encourage these important friendships. She offered to pick up the other girls in her van. Now her daughter gets an extra half hour with her treasured friends, and the mom gets to know her daughter's friends, too.

participating in your activity in order to avoid feeling stuck without a ride later on. You can help resolve this issue by offering to give the student a ride home yourself or by arranging rides for her with other student participants and their parents. If your program starts well after school ends, make sure all students have a safe way of coming and going.

To prevent logistical issues or embarrassment later in the program year or season, be sure to address this topic during orientation or on the first day. Pass around a carpooling sign-up sheet or a list of safe and inexpensive transportation options. (See handout "Car Pool Co-op" on page 85.) If transportation to and from a program or practice is introduced at the outset as an environmentally sensitive way to cut down on traffic, air pollution, and parents' complicated schedules, students who face economic barriers to transportation will feel less singled out and more a part of the broader solution. Promote carpooling, shared bus rides, and group walks as team-building opportunities. Make sure all parents are aware of how their children are getting to and from your practice or program. If you offer new solutions, don't implement them until you receive parents' approval.

Note

[1] Steve Farkas, et al., *Playing Their Parts: Parents and Teachers Talk about Parental Involvement in Public Schools* (New York: Public Agenda, 1999).

Communicating Effectively with Parents

All parents can engage their children in ways that help kids reach their highest potential, whether it's in the classroom, on the sports field, in faith formation programs, on the stage or dance floor, in the music hall, or in many other after-school youth programs and activities. As a parent coordinator, the best way to ensure parents' participation in your youth programming is to clearly communicate your expectations, provide practical strategies, offer developmentally appropriate information, and let parents know how and when they can communicate with you.

Planning Your Communications Strategy

In the month before school and many out-of-school programs start, both kids and their parents become excited (or panicked) as they purchase back-to-school clothes and supplies and start to talk about the upcoming year. Instead of waiting until the start of the program year to think about how you'll communicate with parents, take advantage of the week or two beforehand (one of the best times to catch parents' attention), and let parents know you're available for conversations.

One kindergarten teacher uses this time before school starts to help her former students and their parents connect with their new first-grade teacher and the new school year. In August she sends a note to each of her students from the previous school year. She asks them about their summer and then writes about all the people who will be back at school—the custodian, the principal, the librarian, and other adults they know. She reminds them that their friends will be coming too, and tells them they will have a great year in first grade. One parent says, "This was such great preparation for the school year.

> 66 My son's band instructor has a great system for his practice schedule. He sends home a calendar each semester, and he posts the calendar on the school Web site in case someone loses track of it. 99

BE PREDICTABLE

If you are predictable in the systems you set up, parents are more likely to watch for those messages from you.

- Does your newsletter go home on the same day every week?

- Do you communicate concert and game dates in a letter or on a calendar?

- Do you post the homework assignments online or record them on your phone every night?

This will help parents remember to ask their child for the newsletter you send home every Monday, or to go online each night before asking about homework assignments. If your communication varies, and parents miss the newsletter for several weeks in a row, it ceases to be part of their routine and you will lose their attention. Parents will be much more likely to be engaged in their child's life if they are well informed about what's going on from day to day and week to week.

After reading the note together, I was able to talk with my daughter about how she was feeling about the upcoming year, and we discussed some of the things she was worrying about. I think she is much more relaxed and prepared to start first grade after that note."

Teachers in a number of schools have started making home visits during the month before school starts. These 15-to-20-minute meetings provide an opportunity for teachers and other participating staff to have a conversation with the students and their families and gain perspective on the life their students have outside of school.

Some teachers send a letter home to students to welcome them to their class and tell them and their parents about some of the things they can expect in the upcoming year. (See welcome letters to parents on pages 87–89.) This is a great time to let parents know when they can expect regular communication from you throughout the year. (For example, "Watch for our weekly newsletter on Thursdays. Students help write the newsletter to let you know about our activities during the week.")

Making use of this time before your school or program starts also ensures that your first communication with a family is positive. It is always more difficult if your first conversation with parents is about their son's or daughter's misbehavior.

Identify Systems to Communicate with Families

One of the best forms of communication you can have with parents is face-to-face conversations. While they take time, they are also highly effective in helping parents feel that they are working with you toward success for their son or daughter.

According to a survey conducted by Recruiting New Teachers, Inc., a great way to meet parents in person is to first visit your neighborhood's religious institutions, community center, and library.[1] Once you're familiar with these public areas, you can use them as neutral and nonthreatening meeting spaces where you can engage in conversations with students and their parents. And, of course, meeting at the school or in another public place (even a mall common space) is always an option.

Public meeting spaces will most likely be less intimidating to students and their parents. However, some parents might also be open to having you visit them at home. For example, parents with young children will appreciate not having to find a babysitter or get all of the kids out the door for a school meeting, and parents who work in the evenings might welcome a chance to meet with you on weekends.

Before you call any families, make sure your school district allows teachers or coaches to make home visits. Don't be intimidated by the possibility that some families will say no to your request; it doesn't hurt to ask, and even if they don't feel comfortable with a home visit, they will most likely appreciate the gesture.

Call at least a week before you hope to meet with the family. Even if parents are excited to have you over, they will still appreciate some time to tidy up their home and prepare. Send a reminder card a few days after you've scheduled your meeting. It doesn't have to be anything fancy—just a note card or postcard with the date and time and a comment about how much you're looking forward to the visit. Include your phone number in case they need to cancel or reschedule. (See "Family Visit Reminder" on page 86.)

Another great time to conduct in-home meetings is mid-year when parents and youth have begun to lose momentum. If you live in a colder climate, they may have the winter doldrums, and youth in particular may need a boost to keep them going for the last semester.

Back-to-School Night or Open House

Some teachers note how few parents show up for these early events. Others have high attendance year after year. Here are some strategies that can help you encourage parents to attend and start the school year on a positive note.

Send home multiple invitations, spaced out to serve as reminders.

Be clear about the agenda and the time frame. End the formal event on time to set expectations that parents can count on leaving at the designated time.

Have students prepare a letter to their parent(s) or complete a short writing assignment that their parent will see at the event. Let parents know they'll be seeing something created specifically by their child.

Promise parents that they'll receive a useful resource. This could be a flyer with tips for helping with homework, improving study skills, or planning for postsecondary options; an advance copy of the first newsletter; or some other tip sheet appropriate for the grade level you teach.

The Newsletter

Some teachers still make use of the weekly or monthly paper newsletter that is delivered to parents via their students' backpacks. If this system has worked for you in the past, by all means keep it going, but you might also want to incorporate some new methods as well.

You likely have a number of students who divide their time between two homes, and posting the newsletter on the school Web site is one way to ensure that all parents and guardians have a chance to read the classroom newsletter. Another alternative is to ask parents at the beginning of the year if they would like to receive the newsletter by e-mail. For those who opt for this, create a group e-mail list and send the newsletter on the appointed day.

Some smaller schools send a schoolwide newsletter featuring a section written by each grade or classroom. Any of these options can be effective as long as they convey useful information and are delivered to parents on a predictable schedule.

So, what should go in your newsletter? If your school year is already underway, consider asking a few parents what information they would find most useful in a newsletter. If you are reading this over the summer, consider what information you want parents to have so they feel familiar with your classroom activities and prepared to help their children succeed.

Regular topics to cover might include:

- The classroom schedule.

- Dates of special events for students (class parties, field trips).

- Dates of special events for parents (open houses, conferences, PTA or PTO meetings, special speakers).

- Academic information (test dates, project deadlines, homework assignments). It is helpful to list major deadlines or event dates even if they are far in the future, and then repeat them in the newsletters leading up to the event.

Occasional topics might include:

- A brief article on your (or your school's) philosophy about homework and how much parents and students should expect.

- Basic information about the curriculum you will cover in class, and how parents can support their son or daughter in learning about various topics.

- Articles or references to information about learning styles, test-taking tips, homework strategies, and study skills.

Some teachers make the newsletter a part of their curriculum by having students write brief synopses of activities or topics they have covered in class. All students can participate in the production of the newsletter on a rotating basis. Just make sure to keep the newsletter short enough and simple enough that you can get it out in a timely manner.

You can also make use of newsletters if you are an athletic coach, music director, drama coach, youth program leader, or youth pastor. It may make more sense to create newsletters on a quarterly schedule, rather than on a weekly or monthly basis. You might include a calendar listing upcoming games, performances, field trips, or fundraising events. The newsletter content could include articles on the latest research on properly warming up and cooling down before and after a rigorous athletic practice; features about performances by visiting violinists, bands, or folk groups that students and their parents might be interested in attending; or a column that discusses how to apply faith-based principles to everyday life.

Phone Systems

Technology can enhance your communication with parents. It wasn't that long ago that most schools didn't have phones in individual classrooms or have Web sites and e-mail systems in place. Now, most schools use some or all of these tools to aid in communicating with parents. The challenge is to pick the one or two formats you want to use consistently and design a plan you can stick to.

Phone access and phone systems vary widely by setting. Consider how you can use whatever system is available in order to get critical information to parents.

In some school districts, the athletic department has a recorded telephone message that lists basic information about upcoming sporting events, including dates, times, and locations. Theater groups often do the same. Classroom teachers can use the same strategy to post homework assignments and deadlines for the upcoming week. Some teachers do this by changing their voicemail message every night or week to include this information.

Even if you are already sending the information home in a different format, it can be helpful to have an "on demand" information source for parents. For example, after dinner Joe's mom asks if he has any homework. "I don't know. I don't think so," he says. The newsletter has somehow disappeared into a stack of papers or has been recycled. "Let's call your teacher's phone to check," Joe's mom suggests. An argument is averted and the odds that Joe will complete his homework have just improved.

E-mail

Maybe your voicemail options are limited, or you have assessed your time and preferences and find that e-mail is your best communication option. You can usually build a group e-mail address so that your

My daughter sings in the choir and we nearly missed her last concert because the flyer noted the time of the event and the date, but failed to name a location. I assumed it was at her school, but it was being held at another building in the district. I had to call another family to find out where to go when we got to her school and it was locked.

messages to parents can be sent out quickly. (Be sure to collect parent e-mail addresses at the beginning of the year.) Develop a format or template that ensures that all relevant information is included in every e-mail you send. Consider standardizing a subject line for these e-mails so they don't get lost in the inbox (for example, "Update from Room 212" or "News from the Fighting Cougars"). Place all e-mail addresses in the blind carbon copy (BCC) option of your e-mail system to keep e-mail addresses confidential (and to avoid listing huge groups of addresses that waste paper if printed). Keep in mind that some families don't have access to the Internet, so it's important to use other forms of communication in addition to e-mail.

Parent Account Management Systems

Some districts or schools have formal systems in place that allow parents to access student information, ranging from how much money is left in their child's lunch account to what their child's grades are and whether they have had any disciplinary referrals. If your school has such a system, administrators will talk to you about how to use it. Your best strategy, if you want parents to use it, is to keep information in that system as up to date as possible, and remind them periodically that it is available.

Podcasts

If one of your goals is to keep parents informed about events or topics in your classroom, and you love technology (or are in a district with tech-savvy staff), create podcasts of presentations by you or guest speakers on key topics. Students and parents can access them via the Internet. Perhaps a group at the school or district level can find or develop podcasts on topics that address parents' interests or concerns, such as various curricula, standardized testing procedures, disciplinary processes, college application resources, other school-related topics, or a series of presentations on parenting topics.

Of course, some parents won't have access to the various technologies you include in your communications plan, but if you convey the same information through several channels you will increase the odds that parents will see or hear the information they need to help their children stay on top of schoolwork. And remember, any system you choose is only as good as the information you include. If it's not current and accurate it will do little to help parents contribute to their child's success in school.

Draw Connections to What Matters Most to Parents

One factor that works to your advantage is that parents generally care about how their child is faring in school, on their sports team, in music lessons, and in other extracurricular activities. If you point out the connections between your requests of parents and the desired outcomes for their children, they will be more inclined to read or listen to the messages you send.

For example, tell parents:

I'll be sending homework home on Mondays, Tuesdays, and Thursdays. Math homework is designed to give your child additional practice with the concepts we cover in class. Since we move through the curriculum rather quickly, this practice time allows students to apply the lessons to "real life" problems and gives me a way to see whether they understand the material. It also helps them remember the information in preparation for the standardized tests they will take. You can help by setting up a quiet place for your son or daughter to do homework, ideally around the same time each evening. Your child should be able to complete each assignment in 20 to 30 minutes. If it is routinely taking longer than that, please let me know.

Parents as Homework Partners

To increase the odds that most or all parents will participate in and encourage their children's academic and social development in some way, it is important to communicate directly to them the specific things they can do at home to support what you are doing at school or in your program.

Ask parents to do the following:

Ensure that your child has a quiet spot and a regular time to do homework.

Read to or alongside your child every day. Encourage older children to read to themselves every day and talk to you about what they are reading.

Encourage your child to do his best in his schoolwork and out-of-school activities.

Help your child pack his backpack with paper, pencils, and homework each night, and pack activity bags with books and other equipment for lessons, practices, or rehearsals.

HELP PARENTS PLAN

If you know of major events or units coming up during the year that families might want to plan for, give the necessary information to parents as early as possible.

- For example, if parents know the dates for standardized testing, they will be less likely to schedule dental appointments or family trips during that week.

- If you plan a unit of study requiring students to bring in magazines or other supplies that will take some time to collect, let parents know in advance so they don't have to scramble for materials the night before. ("You need 14 pictures of different bodies of water by *when?*")

> ❝ *My son has trouble with deadlines. His teacher writes a newsletter every month, but lists only the final deadline for projects and not the due dates for the outline, the first draft, and so on. He's always getting docked for missing these interim deadlines, and I can't be much help because I don't have the information I need to help him stay on track.* ❞

BE CONCISE, CLEAR, AND COMPLETE

Your goal in communicating with parents is to make sure they have the information they need to help their child succeed, and to encourage parents' participation by informing them about events and activities. Your written communications don't have to be lengthy; in fact, shorter is often better.

Many parents interviewed for this book mentioned receiving incomplete information as one of their frequent frustrations. To check the completeness of your communication in a memo or newsletter, review the Five Ws of journalism: Who, What, When, Where, and Why. If your description of an upcoming open house, field trip, or other activity covers these points, parents will have the information they need to do their part, whether it's returning a field trip slip on time, showing up for an open house, or ensuring that homework or other projects meet a deadline.

For example, if you send home information about an upcoming field trip, make sure you address the following questions:

- Who is hosting or chaperoning the field trip? Who is responsible for the children's safety and how can they be reached?

- Where are the children going on their field trip?

- When is the field trip? (Include the date and the time children will depart and return if the trip will begin before and end after regular school hours.)

- What does the field trip entail? (Is there a specific subject it will address?) What do parents need to do (sign a permission slip, pay a fee, dress children in particular clothing)?

- Why are the students taking this field trip? (What will they learn? How will they benefit?)

Stress the importance of appropriate behavior outside the home. Role-play and model for your child the respectful language and behavior that should be shown to teachers, coaches, and program leaders.

Work with your child to develop basic social skills. Role-playing and discussing appropriate models on TV and in movies can be helpful ways to illustrate the point.

For more parent tips on supporting children's homework and behavior success, use the handout "Helping Kids with Homework" on page 82.

Extracurricular Activities Communications

What do you do when your athletes, actors and actresses, debaters, singers, or dancers dedicate hours to practice, but their parents don't show support by attending games, plays, debates, concerts, or recitals? First, set up a communication plan for parents, and implement it before the season or program year begins. Most likely, parents would love to attend every event, near and far, but they either don't have sufficient information from you, or don't receive the information far enough in advance to take time off work or schedule a babysitter, or just plain can't make it happen.

As soon as you know important dates, send a calendar of events to parents, and follow up before each event to remind parents. Some parents work evenings or weekends and it may be difficult for them to get time off, and some parents don't live in the same city as their children. All parents will appreciate it if you share with them the monumental dates or events for which they might want to make a special one-time effort to attend. Even if parents can't make it every single time, their children will appreciate their attendance at these special games or events. Also, encourage the kids to remind their parents when something comes up (sometimes children expect their parents to remember everything or to know how important something is to them). Get the kids excited enough that they can't help but run home and tell their parents every detail. It may also go a long way if you talk to the whole group about parent involvement and mention that just because not all parents make it to all events doesn't mean they don't care.

When English Is Not the Primary Language

Parents who struggle to master spoken and written English are at a particular disadvantage when it comes to being fully involved in their children's lives outside the home. While parents may make halting attempts to communicate with language-fluent adults such as employers, neighbors, store clerks, and their children's teachers or youth leaders, their children are rapidly acquiring concepts and language at a pace that leaves parents behind.

Try not to use children as translators for their parents. Ideally, it's best to have an impartial translator who is not related to the parent to preserve a parent's right to privacy. Some school systems provide translators. Realistically, family members may have to interpret for you, but be aware that sometimes interpreters have their own agendas, and may or may not communicate the matter as you are trying to relay it. (See handout "Connect with Language Translators and School Liaisons" on page 91.)

Never assume that your concepts are beyond the comprehension of non-English-speaking parents simply because the language itself is the barrier. Here are a few suggestions for getting beyond that language barrier:

Set aside extra time when you meet with non-English-speaking parents. Avoid giving the impression that you are rushed.

Use paper and pen, an overhead projector, or a whiteboard to sketch a concept or write out your main points, if it's helpful. Sometimes, parents' written comprehension is better than their aural comprehension if they've studied academic English.

Listen carefully, without finishing sentences for parents as they search for a word or phrase. When they are ready for your response, you'll know by their pause.

Look them in the eye as you listen, and offer a smile and facial expression of support and encouragement.

Speak in short sentences, using standard English that communicates one idea at a time.

Try not to use slang terms unless your listener has been "clued in" to the humor and uses of the slang. Remember that all sorts of common expressions, such as "for sure," "she's good to go," or "he's driving me crazy," may not come across well at all!

Realize that you may be a newcomer's most important source of information as an interpreter of the culture or a "cultural broker." Mary Pipher, psychologist and author of *The Middle of Everywhere: Helping Refugees Enter*

OVERCOMING LANGUAGE BARRIERS

Tova Loddigs-Werlinger is a kindergarten teacher at an elementary school where all students are Somali. The school has implemented several practices that foster communication between the school staff, students, and parents. Every two classrooms share an educational assistant who speaks the students' language, and native speakers are on hand to help with parent-teacher conferences.

"We also have Somali people who work in the school office and in administrative positions in the school," Loddigs-Werlinger says. "I think it's important to have this kind of representation at all levels of the school to help parents feel comfortable."

Students are often asked to translate for the teachers or parents, which is not ideal if the parents or teachers need to talk about discipline problems or poor grades. Students may not want to share the whole truth, and the teacher and parents may not realize that they aren't receiving all the facts. Loddigs-Werlinger says impartial translators help take pressure off an uncomfortable discussion and ensure open communication.

"It also helps if the translator is from the community, such as Somali or Hispanic, so if there's a cultural issue the translator can help the teacher or administration understand the cultural differences and make exceptions if needed," Loddigs-Werlinger says.

the American Community, says that teachers are newcomers' most important cultural brokers. Pipher writes that "having a cultural broker can make a tremendous difference in how successfully a new family adapts to America. . . . Every newcomer needs someone who knows how to get things done locally."[2] It's a huge responsibility, but one that can be very rewarding for your students and their families.

If you work with non-English-speaking parents, use the following strategies to help them feel fully included in their child's life (including all classroom, sports, music, theater, or faith-based group events):

- If your school district or program has someone who helps with translation services, find out how they can assist you. If you don't have access to these services, be creative.

- Is there a bilingual parent who is willing to help translate all or part of the newsletter or record homework assignments on your phone message?

- Is there a high school student who is a native speaker or is taking advanced language classes who is willing to help with translation as a service project or to earn extra credit?

Your goal is to help as many parents as possible feel comfortable about working with you and be aware of what is happening with their child while away from home.

Notes

[1] Recruiting New Teachers, Inc., *Connect for Success: Building a Teacher, Parent, Teen Alliance* (Belmont, MA: Recruiting New Teachers, Inc., 2001).

[2] Mary Pipher, *The Middle of Everywhere: Helping Refugees Enter the American Community* (New York: Harcourt, 2003), 94–95.

Reaching Out to Build Positive Relationships with All Parents

All young people want and need to know that their parents care about what is happening in their school or program and expect them to do their best. More than likely, the kids with whom you work come from a variety of socioeconomic, ethnic, cultural, and racial groups. Your goal is to engage all of their parents, regardless of particular life situations. Be sure to welcome all parents warmly, consistently, and without judgment, every time you meet. You'll build their trust gradually, and it can become a transformative factor in the crucial relationship between the home and school or out-of-school setting.

The strategies you use may vary widely and need to be tailored to specific situations, depending upon several factors. In this chapter, you'll find tips for making parent engagement with diverse populations a positive and rewarding experience.

Do parents have older children who have participated in your school or program in past years? Learning curves are considerably shorter when parents are already familiar with your content, ways of doing things, and the expected outcomes for their children.

Are parents familiar with your school or program routines and expectations? Newcomers to the area need time, experience, and education to understand what it is that you are asking them to do. Parent orientation sessions at the beginning of a program year are important. Reach out to invite all parents. Follow up with personal calls and contacts.

Do parents originally come from cultures with different expectations of the roles that parents play in their children's education? It's not uncommon for newcomer parents to think it strange that a teacher or leader would ask them to perform tasks at home that they regard as the teacher's sole responsibility. As the shift continues in the home, school, and workplace from an authoritarian leadership model to an authoritative and collaborative power-sharing model, parents may experience discomfort as differing cultural expectations clash.

Do parents work outside the home? If so, their availability for in-person involvement at school, on the field, or in an out-of-school activity will be limited. However, some employers encourage parents to volunteer in their children's schools and may allow them unpaid time off or a longer, occasional lunch break for specific school-related events such as conferences, performances, and recognition ceremonies. Don't automatically assume working parents won't be available.

Are parents *not* working outside the home? Don't assume they'll be more flexible and available. Some parents are home because they are caring for special-needs children, infants and toddlers, ill parents, or their own health concerns. Others use their home as their workplace and have the same constraints as parents who work away from home.

Are parents' work schedules flexible, or do they have little available time between multiple part-time jobs? It is increasingly common for parents to work two or three jobs to support the family. Realize that they are doing their very best to keep the family afloat and remain as engaged parents within the family, even if they are not physically present in your program or classroom.

Do parents share complex custody arrangements of children? If so, respect the limited time parents are available to be with their child in your setting. Ask parents for detailed contact information that allows you to reach them during the time their child is in your program or classroom. Also ask them to clarify how they communicate with each other so that you can ensure a clear path for communication of the same material to each parent.

Are some parents new to this country and to the language and social customs in your area? It's possible that newcomers may not have had the same educational opportunities as their peers, or that their educations may have been interrupted by social forces outside their control. Also, parents may be unfamiliar with school or community routines that you take for granted. On the other hand, the educational levels and technical achievements of some newcomer parents may far exceed the demands of their current employment situation. They may lack licensing credentials and mastery of spoken and written English that are required to land a similar position in their new country. Whatever you do, don't make unfounded assumptions about their ability to engage with their child's learning activities.

You can be successful in involving parents in each of these diverse circumstances with careful advance planning, and by keeping in mind the following:

- Communicate your goals through a variety of channels.

- Emphasize that one of your most important goals is to establish caring one-on-one relationships among parents, children, and yourself.

- Listen to parents' concerns and act on them. Then communicate the results promptly.

When Families Have Limited Resources

Often, parents are hindered in their efforts to participate in their children's schools or program activities by personal financial struggles. Transportation can be a huge issue: cars are expensive, auto insurance doubly so, and finding rides or public transportation on a schedule that meshes with your program needs and their home schedules may be very difficult. Childcare is another significant hurdle for parents with younger children. Appropriate clothing may be yet another issue. Parents may feel they do not have the right apparel to wear in public and may feel intimidated if their past experiences have been negative. Try these strategies to address parents' difficulties:

Are some parents willing to provide rides to other parents who have no cars? Identify volunteer drivers among the parents of kids in your program or class who can be "on call" as needed when other parents' transportation issues arise. Give your parent drivers a valid address, telephone number, correct pronunciation of the name of the parent they are to pick up, and the pickup time. Be sure to have the driver call and confirm the pickup time and place with the parent receiving the ride in order to avoid any delay or confusion.

Can parents ride the school bus with their children to attend a special school program? Check with your transportation scheduler to see whether this is an option.

Can you schedule events flexibly so that parents have some control over timing? When you plan parent-child-teacher conferences, be sure to offer a first, second, and third choice of time on a conference preference sheet, and then do your best to honor the parent's choices. Be sure to clearly communicate the appointment time with families and call parents to confirm any last-minute changes. If you leave a message, ask that the parent return your call to let you know they understand the change. Follow up on any messages that are not confirmed.

Can you provide childcare on-site so that siblings have a safe place to play? Some parents would be delighted to volunteer in their child's classroom or program if only they had affordable and available childcare for younger siblings in the family. Some middle school and high school Family and Consumer Science (FACS) classes have curriculum units that involve hands-on childcare components. Check with the teachers of those programs to set up scheduled childcare or nursery school hours for families who need it. If your program has access to an open gym, playground, or play area that is ideal for sibling care, obtain permission to staff it with volunteer parents on a rotating basis.

Can you provide the basics of hospitality for every parent? Cups, napkins, water, coffee, and crackers at a parent check-in point provide a no-frills, yet adequate, offering of food and drink that goes a long way toward increasing parents' physical comfort. Be sure to indicate safe places for parents to leave their personal belongings and show them where adult restrooms are located.

Can you meet parents off-site at their housing area? Some apartment buildings have community rooms that are available as neutral and convenient spaces for meeting with parents. Other public places such as public libraries, city halls, churches, and fire departments offer free meeting space. Coffee shops and playgrounds are good meeting spots as well.

Community Models for Successful Parent Relationship Building

A number of communities and organizations across the country have developed successful strategies that make it possible for more parents to be fully engaged in their child's education and able to feel empowered and entrusted with the responsibility for helping their children succeed. You'll find a number of inspiring ideas here that are worth replicating.

Colorado Statewide Parent Coalition, Westminster, Colorado

The Colorado Statewide Parent Coalition believes that "parent involvement is the key that opens the door for children's success in school." The coalition has been working for more than 26 years to provide a statewide forum where parents can come together and learn in a friendly, nonthreatening environment. The coalition's Web site, www. coparentcoalition.org, offers a number of resources for both parents and professionals seeking to more effectively engage parents in their child's education.

The coalition recognizes that Hispanic/Latino parents bring many cultural strengths to American society, including the value they place on education as a path to opportunity for their children. It takes into account that traditionally, Hispanic/Latino parents admire teachers and respect teachers' authority, but may not realize that active parent participation in their child's school is wanted or even expected. Additionally, the notion of extended family is very important. It is common for children to live at home beyond high school graduation, and it is expected that children and teens will help their family. Gender roles may be more traditional, although this is changing.

To avoid misunderstandings, it is important to communicate to parents your expectations for their children and to describe the curriculum you will be using. Let parents know about your homework policies. Your approach to homework assignments and completion may be different from their past experience.

Increasingly, schools and programs are challenged to provide translations of materials into other languages and may establish informal networks of volunteer or paid translators and liaisons.

Project Cornerstone, Santa Clara County, California

Project Cornerstone is an asset-building initiative that works throughout Santa Clara County, California, to recruit adults in helping develop asset-building opportunities for young people. One of Project Cornerstone's goals has been to effectively engage parents in their children's schools. The county's overall population of 1.7 million is 39 percent white, 30 percent Asian, and 26 percent Hispanic/Latino. More than 45 percent of all households in the county speak a language other than English at home.[1]

Linda Silvius, the school partnership director for Project Cornerstone, is passionate about bringing parents into active association with their children's schools. One of her tasks is to introduce the 40 Developmental Assets to all parents. She ensures that printed materials for parents are available in English, Spanish, and Vietnamese.

At one point, a group of Spanish-speaking parents expressed an interest to Silvius in learning more about Search Institute's Developmental Assets framework. She hired a professional translator to rewrite *Taking Asset Building Personally* (Search Institute, 1999) in Spanish. The book, a guide for parents and group leaders, formed the basis for discussion with a small number of parents. Interest in learning more

WHERE DO I GO FROM HERE?

Do you work with families who are not native English speakers? Borrow these strategies for successful involvement of *all* families from the Colorado Statewide Parent Coalition (www.coparentcoalition.org):

- Recognize that the extended family is considered a particular strength in many newcomer families. Extend invitations to school performances to family members other than parents to involve the whole family.

- Ask if an older sibling or close relative can help with homework assignments if a parent is not available when a child arrives home from school.

- Help students feel connected and safe in your classroom. Ask parents about cultural customs and learn about their experiences. This encourages parents to feel more comfortable with the school as well.

- Make an effort to send written materials home in the family's native language (Spanish and other languages, if possible and appropriate), as well as in English. Identify resources in your district—ranging from formal translation services to high school language students who volunteer to assist you—to make translation possible.

WHERE DO I GO FROM HERE?

Do you use Search Institute's Developmental Assets framework in your work with children and families? Then consider these asset-based action strategies from Project Cornerstone of San Jose, California:

- Invite parents to your school or organization to teach them about the Developmental Assets.

- If you work with non-English-speaking families, print parent materials in parents' primary language as well as English. Enlist the help of a text translator. You can ask a volunteer to complete the translation as a pro bono project. It also helps to have a translator available for the meeting to interpret your words and answer questions.

- After the Developmental Assets training session ends, ask for parent volunteers to lead the next session of their peers, and provide them with materials and a space to meet.

about the Developmental Assets eventually spread to several hundred parents across Santa Clara County.

Now, Silvius and her staff members go into schools to lead the initial group discussion and introduction to the Developmental Assets. At the conclusion of the first session, they recruit volunteers to be trained as leaders for the next group session. Recruiting parents to continue the group discussion with their peers enables parents to share their understanding of Developmental Assets with each other and sustains the group's ongoing work at each school site over the long term.

One group of Spanish-speaking parents asked how they could apply their knowledge of the Developmental Assets, and Silvius turned to the work of Assets for Colorado Youth (ACY). She followed the example of an asset-building project that ACY had developed called *Los Dichos de La Casa*—stories from the home. In Mexican culture, adults commonly use pithy sayings or *dichos* to transmit important cultural ideas to their children. In Colorado, parents were asked to identify the *dichos* that were commonly quoted in their own homes as they were growing up. ACY compiled the *dichos* into booklets and organized the sayings according to the Developmental Asset they complemented.

Eventually, Project Cornerstone purchased bilingual children's books with themes that reflected each of the assets. Parents receive training to read and use the books with their children and then become volunteers in their children's classrooms, where they are able to use a lesson or script to guide them as they read and discuss the books. Once a month, parents share a culturally appropriate story with the children. They read a page from the story in Spanish, and the teacher follows by reading a page in English. Afterward, parent volunteers lead a short discussion and participate in an activity with the students.

Assets for Colorado Youth, Denver, Colorado

Assets for Colorado Youth (ACY), the leader for Developmental Asset–building across the state of Colorado, helped Denver-area schools address their goal of improving parent engagement in the schools. Schools not only wanted to increase the number of parents who volunteered, but also hoped to create systems and structures within schools that would support sustained parent engagement.

The Expect Success Project was started in two elementary schools, two middle schools, and one high school within the same school system, representing close to 4,000 students. On average, the student population was 85 percent Latino and 7 percent white, with the remainder identifying as Asian, African American, and American Indian.

An external evaluation of the project focused on the following key findings:

- Parent engagement needs to be seen as an *enhancement* to the work done by teachers to support academic achievement.

- Within individual schools, there is a wide range of definitions of parent engagement, which can often be a barrier in connecting with parents.

- Teachers and principals need to agree upon the key components of parent engagement.

- Communication is *crucial* between school staff members, between parents and children, and between schools and parents.

- A positive school climate supports effective parent engagement, and effective parent engagement enhances a positive school climate.

- Any efforts to create a welcoming climate for increased parent engagement need to include school staff members and parents, both simultaneously and separately.

Over the four-year span of the project, ACY staff members were available to teach school personnel many strategies to engage different groups of parents. In addition, they worked with staff members to improve school climate issues.

In early conversations, ACY found that some school staff members held negative perceptions about parents. Teachers didn't want parents in their classrooms and felt that if a child was not successful, it was because the child's parent didn't care. At the other end of the spectrum were staff members who expressed positive impressions of parents and saw their joint relationship as a true partnership on behalf of the children. Over time, conversations that ACY held with teachers and administrators allowed the school personnel to air their concerns and hear other points of view from their colleagues, which sometimes led to new behaviors that were more parent-friendly.

School Success Initiative, Hennepin County, Minnesota

Hennepin County, Minnesota, is a densely populated county composed of the city of Minneapolis and a number of suburban communities. The Hennepin County Human Services and Public Health Department runs the School Success Initiative, the goal of which is to

WHERE DO I GO FROM HERE?

Do you work in a school? Try these parent engagement strategies from Assets for Colorado Youth (www.buildassets.org):

- Assess the overall school climate. Are teachers happy? What about the students and administration? Have there been any long-term issues?

- Gauge the level of parent involvement. How often are parents present in classrooms, in the cafeteria, on the playground, at extra-curricular events, at fundraisers?

- Evaluate student achievement levels and attitudes. What grades do students in your classroom earn? How are attendance and tardiness? Is homework being turned in on time and done to a satisfactory level?

- Make a concerted effort to reach out to parents if you find that the overall school climate seems negative, or parents don't have a physical presence in the school, or students aren't working to the best of their abilities. Try the following:

  - Organize town hall–style meetings so they can voice their opinions and concerns.

  - Invite parents to meet with you one-on-one.

WHERE DO I GO FROM HERE?

Do you work in an urban setting? Try some of these strategies from Hennepin County, Minnesota's School Success Initiative:

- Set one main goal for parent involvement so that you can identify all the smaller goals that will help you succeed.

- Show an interest in learning more about the family's culture if it differs from your own.

- Go beyond youth-centered resources and offer information geared toward parents on job training, employment options, and continuing education.

- Visit parents at their homes, community centers, or religious institutions instead of always meeting at the school or program site.

ensure all children graduate from high school. Parent engagement is one of the initiative's four areas of strategic focus.

Staff members for the initiative represent the communities to which outreach is particularly directed. One staff member works with Hispanic/Latino parents in downtown Minneapolis, as well as in the suburbs. Parents tell her that they want their children to do well in school, and want to do what they can to support their children's successes. They are happy when schools make an effort to understand their culture, especially when efforts go beyond "one more piñata party at school." Hispanic/Latino parents appreciate their children's school staff members making efforts to create an atmosphere of trust. They also comment that parents teach other parents what they have learned about working "within the system" and that parent-to-parent education can be very effective.

The School Success Initiative staff member who works as a liaison with the African American community has found that in the inner city, parents want living wage jobs and skills development for themselves as well as for their children. Once parents are admitted to job training programs and are actively engaged in their own learning, they are motivated to reinforce the importance of learning in their own families.

School Success Initiative staff members working in each community identified several key strategies that lead to deeper parent engagement: teachers and leaders listening to parents, sometimes going to where parents *are* instead of always expecting parents to come to the school, and learning more about the family's culture.

When working across cultures, remember that all parties can learn something new. Parents don't expect that you will already know everything about their culture. When you express a genuine interest in learning more, parents are more likely to see you as someone they can trust. Learning to work cross-culturally is a positive challenge, and one that can be rewarding as you make lasting connections to families.

Establishing a Strong Program-Home Connection

Thousands of TV, radio, and Internet commercials, as well as a stack of direct mail, compete daily for parents' attention. In many families, the flood of communications that comes into the home is quite substantial. On top of that, some of the families you are trying to reach are not fluent readers or speakers of English. Simply grabbing parents' attention about your program is a real challenge.

When it comes right down to it, you only have so many hours a week to work with youth—they spend the majority of their time outside your classroom or program with their families and elsewhere. You probably agree that your job is a lot easier when you can maximize the time you are with kids rather than having to make up for lost time that could have been used at home. One of your goals, then, is to help parents understand the importance of things they can do at home to support their children's learning, artistic and creative development, physical fitness, and constructive activities.

Although you may think you have little control over what goes on in your students' lives beyond your classroom, team, or youth program, you *can* have an impact on what they are able to accomplish at home by communicating clearly and regularly with parents. Let parents know what their children are working on or practicing. You can share effective strategies that parents can use at home when trying to reinforce homework, sports or music practice, or completion of special projects.

If a young person is having problems, communicate your concerns to her parents immediately rather than waiting until a formal meeting time. If your communications are consistent and timely, parents will be less likely to feel attacked or blindsided, and, most important, the student will benefit from prompt help.

In the same vein, don't save success stories for a formal meeting! Parents will be delighted to hear that their child had an improved score on a math quiz, was able to run an extra lap in track, or finally remembered all of the lyrics in a big choir solo. Since you most likely can't get in touch with every parent each time something positive happens, send a note now and then that sums up how well things have been going for each child.

Communication should be two-way. In addition to reporting concerns and successes to parents, be sure to ask them plenty of questions about their child. Parents have incredible insight into their own child's temperament, learning styles, and basic likes and dislikes. They will almost certainly appreciate the interest you take in getting to know their child. Instead of their child being just another body in your classroom, after-school program, or sports, speech, or drama team, they will know you genuinely care about each individual and will be more likely to continue open communication with you. They will be as excited to share home-based successes with you as you are to share successes that occur under your leadership.

CREATING HARMONY WITH "EXTRACURRICULAR" PARENTS

Peter Dotson has taught guitar lessons to children and teens for five years. He often has a harder time dealing with his students' parents than the students themselves. "Parents want everything to be easy," he says, so he tries to make things as simple for them as possible. "They work so much anyway, they'd rather not have to coax their child into practicing."

Dotson does have students who don't practice between lessons. He thinks the best thing a teacher can do to make learning an instrument easier on parents is to instill in the child a love of playing it.

"I do subtle coaching to get the student to practice, but when they get to choose their area of study—rock, blues, classical, metal— it's usually no problem," he says. "I advise parents that a practice regimen of short, regular practices is far better than single sessions of longer duration. When a parent approaches me about getting their child to practice, it signals me that I need to change my instructional approach to better engage the child."

Some parents choose guitar study for their child, rather than allowing the child to make the choice. Dotson's advice to parents is not to push their children into an activity in which they don't have a genuine interest. His most rewarding experiences as a teacher are with students who truly love the art of guitar and have a passion for learning to play.

"Sometimes parents try to live vicariously through their children, pushing them to be rock stars," Dotson says. "Kids aren't going to want to practice during the week if they don't really want to play guitar."

Dotson tries to help parents keep things in perspective by encouraging them to be excited for their children and less serious about the whole process. "I tell them that their kids are just that—kids," he says.

Strong Networks for Parents

A final strategy in building relationships with parents is to find opportunities for them to get to know each other. Whether it's planning a quarterly coffee time in the lunchroom with the principal and other staff members, or scheduling parents to work together in groups rather than solo, opportunities for parents to get to know each other are highly beneficial for them and for students.

In the short run, knowing other parents reinforces the process of supporting kids' learning and encourages volunteering. In the larger scheme of things, parents who sometimes feel isolated discover that chatting with other parents helps them feel less alone, and provides opportunities to exchange parenting tips and other information.

As children grow older and become more autonomous, it becomes harder for parents to connect with parents of their children's classmates. Relationships formed while children are young help parents feel more comfortable calling each other in future years, whether it is to make sure there will be an adult present at a party, or to see if "all the other parents" are really letting their kids go to an event. The relationships you encourage, nurture, and sustain among parents can lead to lifelong community connections that strengthen your program, children's successes, and parents' sense of identity and belonging in the community.

Note

[1] U.S. Census Bureau, State and County QuickFacts, Santa Clara County, California, retrieved April 3, 2008, from quickfacts.census.gov.

Meeting Parents
One-on-One

Demands on your time are many and varied. It may seem more efficient to meet with parents in groups whenever possible. However, meeting with parents one-on-one is often the most effective way to reach a common understanding of the issues facing their own child and the best strategies for addressing those issues.

All parents believe their child is unique. They want other adults to see their child in a positive light. They want their child to receive all the help they need to be successful in school and in life. They typically see their child in the context of the family, and may not have accurate perceptions about how their child compares to others of the same age or how their child gets along in a larger group of peers.

Teachers, youth group leaders, youth pastors, and coaches *do* get to know students individually, but most often interact with them as part of a group. Teachers have a prescribed curriculum to impart to students over a fixed period of time. Sports coaches set goals they want the team to reach, such as winning games, improving performance times, and mastering new skills. Drama coaches aim to teach performance and timing skills, music and movement, blocking, and choreography to members of their cast.

In any group of young people, some will already know or quickly understand the content and may already have the necessary skills and experience for your subject area or program. Others will take longer—they may struggle with or even fail to reach set goals in the available time.

In addition, some youth arrive with personal skills such as perseverance, the ability to take turns and share, and a willingness and ability to follow directions. Others may struggle with learning disabilities, psychological challenges, or occasional life crises that make behaviors such as impulse control or waiting their turn beyond their reach. You will need to prepare parents for these variables and emphasize the need to exercise patience and a nonjudgmental attitude as they work with kids in the group. The intent is to ensure that every student learns to the best of his ability and can enjoy participating!

Sometimes parents have quite a different view of their child from that of teachers, program leaders, or coaches. Finding ways to communicate while meshing these divergent views can be a challenge. But honest communication gives all parties a clearer picture of the child as an individual and as a learner, and can form the basis for a plan of action in which each adult has a role to play in supporting the child.

Whenever you're working with groups of young people, it is necessary to strike a delicate balance between expectations for all students and appropriate accommodations for individuals. Only through communication does a clear path emerge.

One-on-One: Parent-Teacher-Student Conferences

While there may be opportunities for one-on-one communication early in the school year, often the first time parents and teachers engage in a one-on-one conversation is during student performance conferences. These are key opportunities to meet parents and engage them in their child's educational progress. Conferences can be (and often are) stressful for both parents and teachers, but they can also be excellent opportunities to identify what's working for a student and which areas need additional effort.

Generally, schools set the basic parameters for the conference format. Your first step is to think about the format used by your school, and to decide how you can make conferencing most effective for each child's parents and for your own needs. An innovative and increasingly common way to encourage parent participation is to hold a student-led conference, in which students not only participate, but also turn to their parents and explain in their own words what their schoolwork and test scores mean, with the assistance of their teachers.

Conferences may take place "arena-style" in the gymnasium, media center, or cafeteria, with teachers seated at tables and parents standing in line in "first-come, first-served" order to speak to their child's teachers. Conferences may also take place in the privacy of individual classrooms, with parents signing up in advance for a time slot. Your school may or may not encourage or require students to participate in the conferences.

Conference Communications

One of the first and most basic things you can do to make conference time effective is to ensure that parents know when conferences will take place and how they will be structured.

Be sure to send home to parents a choice of times and dates that they can consider for the upcoming meeting. In addition to a letter with information on dates and the location for conferences, what else can you send home beforehand to help parents prepare? A note in your newsletter, a flyer, or an e-mail can outline your philosophy of conferencing and what you hope to provide during the time you spend together, as well as explain what parents and children can do to prepare. You can also send home a preconference planner that both parent and child fill out together to focus their thoughts and goals for the meeting. See the handout "A Parent's Conference Planner" on page 94 for an example.

During the Conference

Let's look at the conference process in detail. Consider giving parents the handout "A Parent's Guide: Questions to Ask during the Conference" on page 95 to help them take notes during the conference. Begin with an area in which the young person is doing well. Reflect on the school year to date. Are there areas of growth you have observed? Are there characteristics about the student as a learner that you appreciate? For example:

He's interested in everything. He asks good questions that let me know he is really paying attention. At first I thought he might be trying to steer the class off the topic, but I now see that he is trying to understand multiple aspects of the topic we are discussing.

She's always on time and ready to learn. She remembers to bring her materials to class and pays attention to the lesson.

He's a bundle of energy. He throws himself into every classroom activity. I've moved him to the front of the room where his energy can be directed at me and not the students around him. In small group work I team him with several students who are more reserved, because he is good at engaging them in conversation.

Next, highlight specific academic accomplishments. Go beyond a review of assignments and test grades. Numerous parents interviewed for this book felt their child's teacher didn't really "know" their child. When pressed for an example, several said, "At conferences, all the teacher did was show me my child's grades. It didn't seem as though the teacher knew anything else about my child." It doesn't take a lot of extra conversation to show parents you have a genuine interest in their child.

For example:

Last week we finished a unit on weather. She put a lot of time into her final project, and it was very well done. Her artwork really added a lot to the report.

He's been working hard on his spelling. Even though he is just learning English, he is doing a good job and each week he does a little better. He scored 100 percent on the last two spelling quizzes. I can tell he is putting in time outside class to master the words.

She wrote a thoughtful essay on democracy last month. Her first draft contained grammar errors, but her final draft was very well done. I know she put a lot of time and effort into making corrections and polishing it.

This can be a good place to ask parents for feedback on how their child is feeling about school. Ask parents to share their thoughts and questions from the preconference form and ask them for their perspective on the year so far.

Both parents and you can identify specific ways to help support the development of their child's strengths. In addition to providing a way to focus on strengths, parent-teacher conferences encourage parents and teachers to work together to help the young person develop in healthy ways. Too often, the relationship between parent and teacher can feel distant or even adversarial.

Creating opportunities to speak positively about ways to work together can help parents be more comfortable with and confident in their child's educational experience. At the conclusion of the conference, offer parents a list of action items and suggestions for organizing school materials. See the handout "Getting Organized after the Parent-Teacher Conference" on page 96.

In some conferences you may feel as though you and the parent are talking about two different people. Could this charming, eager child the parents are describing be the same student who sits slumped in her desk and refuses to answer your questions? Could this child described as respectful at home be the same student who seems unaware of social rules and is constantly getting in trouble with another child in the classroom? Could this child who is oppositional at home and refuses to help with chores be the same student who volunteers consistently to help in the classroom?

Rather than assuming one perspective is right and the other is wrong, use one-on-one meetings as an opportunity to put more of the pieces of the puzzle together and to collaborate to identify positive strategies everyone can use. Starting with a focus on the positives can open the door to a productive conversation.

It helps to remember that young people's lives are experienced across multiple contexts. The first and most influential factor in their development is their family. Some children rarely venture outside the family circle until they begin formal schooling. Others may have had experiences with daycare or preschool or large groups of cousins or neighbor children and have learned to navigate in larger social circles.

As children grow, and particularly toward the end of the elementary years and beginning of the middle school years, their peer group becomes a more potent influence. If they have a group of friends who all like school and do well academically, this will positively influence their feelings and behaviors around schooling. If their friends are struggling with school, or have had a series of negative experiences in school, then this peer influence will pull them away from positive messages about school and its importance.

Their teachers and other school personnel have also contributed to their perceptions of themselves as learners and their ideas of what school is all about.

On top of that, parents have their own personal experiences with schooling. For some, it brings back happy memories. For others, school was something to be endured until it was possible to escape. When you, the parent(s), and the student meet for a conference, these past experiences are "present" as well. Setting the stage for a collaborative conference can help put everyone at ease.

As you prepare for conferences, consider your core assumptions about learning. Do any of the following spring to mind? The following examples reflect a wide variety of beliefs:

- **Every student can learn,** although some students may take longer to master a body of knowledge.

- **There are many types of learners.** It's key to find out what type of learner each student is. Different activities help different types of learners succeed.

> " *My father was a high school dropout. I actually had some of the same teachers he had in school. He made a point of communicating with my teachers about how proud he was of me, and let them know that he placed a higher value on education for his children than he did as a student himself.* "

COMBATING HOMEWORK STRESS

One 4th grader was so overwhelmed by the amount of homework he had each night that homework time became stressful for the whole family. It often resulted in arguments with his parents and ultimately not completing his assignments.

His mother e-mailed his teacher and explained the situation—her son was burned out and frequently procrastinated. She said he had no time to do other things, such as read for pleasure, and she didn't believe this was healthy.

His teacher responded with many possible solutions to his homework woes. He could:

- Do homework for a set amount of time each evening.

- Alternate certain assignments; for example, he could do his geography homework one week and his history homework the next.

- Work on a lighter load of homework; for example, the teacher could assign shorter spelling lists.

She also invited the student and his parents to meet with her in person. She used a brainstorming technique to open up a discussion about homework, a form she had titled "A Totally Awesome Homework Plan!" (See the handout on page 97.) Under the first question, "What is homework time like now?" he and his parents wrote "stressful." The teacher then asked what their goals were—how did he *want* homework time to feel?

After identifying that he wanted his homework time to be fun and peaceful, he decided to spend 40 minutes on homework each night—no more, no less—and when the 40 minutes were up, he was done with his homework, even if the assignments weren't actually complete.

The teacher's flexibility around homework really paid off for the 9-year-old. He doesn't

cont'd

- **School provides a socializing experience for students.** It is important for students to learn skills that help them get along with others and behave respectfully.

- **Academic achievement is the core responsibility of the school and the teacher.** Mastering a body of knowledge is the most critical activity that happens in schools.

- **Parents may push their children too hard, or not enough,** may be overly engaged in their child's schoolwork or entirely disinterested in it, and may be strong advocates for our school, or are difficult to deal with and always questioning what we do.

Where did you land? Did any of your responses surprise you? Do these beliefs affect the way you organize your classroom? How do you think your opinions affect your approach to parent-teacher conferences? Think about the beliefs you want to share with parents so they understand how you envision the classroom experience and your role as a teacher. Even if your beliefs differ from theirs, talking about your perspectives can help you start building a relationship with them. Even if their prior experiences with teachers have been less than positive, your efforts can help turn that impression around.

Discussing Student Behavior

Talking about problems a student is having can be difficult. Parents may be disappointed, frustrated, in denial, angry, ashamed, or embarrassed. Focus on the specific behaviors rather than attributing general characteristics to the student's personality.

For example, say, "He interrupts other students when I have called on them to answer a question" rather than, "He's always disruptive in class." Or, "She hasn't turned in any math homework for the last three weeks" rather than, "She's lazy."

This allows you and the student's parents to focus on strategies for changing the problematic behavior, rather than focusing on whether the child is disruptive at heart, or lazy, and so on.

Name the strategies you are using to try to shape the behavior. Ask the student's parents whether there are situations in which they have observed the same behavior. In some cases they may have ideas for how to address the behavior, or they may be able to identify some stressful event that has triggered a particular behavior. For example, parents might respond that the student hasn't been able to focus on schoolwork because she's worried about her grandmother, who has been hospitalized for the past month, and that she is helping around the house so her parents can be at the hospital.

With everyone's input, you can suggest additional strategies you might plan to use, or ask them whether they can use some of the same strategies at home to reinforce a new behavior. "I'll make a point of having a conversation with her and let her know that I am sorry to hear her grandmother is ill. I'll work with her on a plan to make up portions of each missed homework assignment and see if she would like to spend part of her lunch hour working in my room so she can get help on any concepts she's forgotten. Can you work with her to spend a half-hour each evening on her current assignments so she doesn't fall behind?"

If there is time, you can comment on any specific strategies you recommend all parents use. "Spelling tests are always on Fridays. I'm asking all parents to spend five or ten minutes at breakfast or dinner to go over the spelling words and post the list on the refrigerator as a reminder." If you know the conference time is limited, consider creating handouts with some of these general tips to give to parents at conference time.

After you've had a chance to discuss any questions they might have for you or vice versa, draw the conference to a close by commenting on something positive about the student and sharing your hopes for the next term.

For example, say, "I'll talk with him to get his input on why he is interrupting other students. I think he can change this behavior if we all work together to reinforce the times when he lets other students speak in class. I will let you know how it is going, so you can encourage him as well."

Unscheduled Parent Meetings

Teachers put in long hours before and after school, and they also need to make use of every minute they have in the classroom. It is not surprising, therefore, that teachers don't appreciate having parents show up unannounced with "just a quick question," which is often the start of a longer conversation. These unscheduled one-on-one meetings can go better if you set expectations early. In your newsletter or at back-to-school night, offer the best times and ways to reach you.

Throughout the year, issues pop up and need attention. Ideally you will already have asked parents to indicate on a form (at an open house or conferences) how and when they prefer to be contacted. Keeping parents in the loop and engaging them in the process early

fight homework anymore, and whereas completing an assignment used to mean three hours of arguing and procrastination, it now means 40 solid minutes of focused concentration.

"Ironically, he finishes most of his homework," his mother says.

The whole process made the 4th grader feel powerful, his mother says. He loved that his teacher and parents listened to what he thought and that he was allowed to take part in the solution to his problem. It really made a difference that his teacher cared about him and sincerely wanted him to love school. His mother believes the teacher's caring attitude mattered even more to her son than the new approach to homework.

on helps them feel part of the solution. If you are the person initiating the conversation, be mindful of the other person's time and be clear about what you need to communicate. You are most likely to contact a parent when a problem has arisen. To build trust and optimism, you might want to build "positive contacts" into your routine so not all mid-year conversations are centered around a problem.

Some teachers keep a stack of postcards or note cards in their desk and use downtime—perhaps when students are reading or taking a test—to write one or two notes to parents to let them know their child did something good. Sometimes it is focused on a behavior:

> *She has been very helpful to a new student who just joined our class last week. I have really appreciated how she has gone out of her way to sit by him, show him where things are in the building, and walk with him in the halls.*

> *He noticed that the locker room was a mess after the last game. He took the initiative to ask his teammates to help clean it up before they left so the custodian wouldn't be left with all the work.*

Sometimes it is focused on academics:

> *She has completed all her assignments on time this week. I can tell that she is really trying to stay on top of her schoolwork.*

> *He delivered a great presentation in class today. He made PowerPoint slides to accompany his speech and did a good job answering his classmates' questions.*

While these notes don't take long to do, they have a huge impact on parents. All parents love to hear that their child is doing something well. The notes also give parents a peek into their child's classroom.

Consider sending a letter at the beginning of the year that states something like this: "During the day I need to attend to teaching, so unfortunately I won't have time for conversations with parents who drop by. However, you can leave me a voicemail during the day, and I will try to return it after school that day or before school the next day. If you need to see me in person, the best times to try to schedule a meeting are Thursdays before school (7:15 to 8:15) or Tuesdays and Thursdays after school (between 3:30 and 4:30.) If e-mail works for you, I try to check mine every evening. My phone number is ____ and my e-mail address is ____."

One-on-one meetings with parents can be productive and positive experiences if you let parents know how best to reach you and when you are generally available. Remember, you and parents are partners in helping students learn.

One parent had this to say about her son's teacher: "I know she must be really busy with all the students she has, but she took time to send me a note when my son did something good in class. I know he's pretty rambunctious and can't be the easiest kid to have in class, but when I went to conferences I got the sense that she genuinely liked him. She has given me a couple of easy strategies that I can use at home to reinforce what she is doing in the classroom to help him settle down. They really work, too. This has been a great year for him. I can tell he really likes school for the first time."

5

Icebreakers for Group Gatherings

An effective strategy for both recruiting and retaining parent volunteers is to build interactive activities into gatherings you have for parents. Parents who have fun together and who get to know you and each other are more comfortable visiting your school, classroom, or meeting location, and are more comfortable working with you and with each other. Conversely, parents who don't get to know other parents or staff will find it harder to come back for events or to volunteer.

Just as you spend time at the beginning of the school or program year building rapport among young people, be sure to spend some time at the beginning of any conversation with a parent or gathering of parents getting to know them and letting them get to know each other. This can be as simple as making sure you have name tags for parents at all events, and making time for parents to go around the group introducing themselves—or, if the group is very large, at least making time for them to introduce themselves to the parent on either side of them.

In addition to these basic strategies, you can also include structured group activities to create a positive experience for parents who attend meetings. As you use the activities that follow, adapt them depending on the parents you are working with, the size of the group, the time you have available, and your goals for the event.

1. Name Tag Sandwich

Suggested Group Size: Any size

Estimated Time: 5 minutes

Materials: name tags; pens or markers

Directions:

1. As participants fill out their name tags, ask them to write their name in the middle and leave space on the bottom and top of their name tag. Ask them to write on the top the name of someone who had a positive impact on their life. Ask them to write on the bottom the name of their child or children.

2. After parents have filled out their name tags and put them on, ask them to walk around the room (or turn to the person next to them if the seating is crowded), introduce themselves, and talk about the person who had a positive influence on them, and how they want to be a positive influence on their own child.

2. Parenting Bingo

Suggested Group Size: 12–100

Estimated Time: 12–15 minutes

Materials: Parenting Bingo handout (page 99) (one for each person); pens; six or eight small prizes (such as a refrigerator magnet, candy bar, or an item related to your school or program)

Directions:

1. Form teams of four to eight people. Give each person a Parenting Bingo sheet and pen. Have the entire group play Parenting Bingo— collecting signatures of individuals who fit the description in each box. The goal for participants is to completely fill a row, column, or diagonal. If the group is large enough, specify that each person should sign the sheet only once. Allow about 10 minutes.

2. Reconvene the small teams to count the total number of signatures for their group. Award the winning team members a small prize. If groups are not of equal size, have teams figure out the average number of signatures per team member.

Tip for Success: Make sure the room you're using is large enough to allow comfortable mingling.

3. Grand Pandemonium

Suggested Group Size: Any size

Estimated Time: 12 minutes

Materials: Grand Pandemonium handout (page 100) and pens for everyone in the group

Directions: Ask participants to follow the directions on the handout "Grand Pandemonium" (page 100), collecting signatures as they complete the tasks.

4. Two-by-Two — Answering Questions with a Partner

Suggested Group Size: Any size

Estimated Time: (under 5 minutes—about 2 minutes per question)

Materials: None

Directions: Even if you have only a few minutes to devote to an icebreaker, those minutes are time well spent. Whether your group is large or small, you can ask people to form pairs and give them one of the following questions to talk about with each other:

Question: Who has influenced you to become the adult you are today? What did they do?

Question: Name a person (who is not a celebrity) you consider a hero and why.

Question: Think about a time when you learned something that was really interesting to you. It doesn't have to be something you learned in school. What was it?

Question: If you and your child could spend an afternoon together anywhere in the world, where would it be and what would you want to do together?

Question: What is the most important lesson you hope to pass on to your child(ren)? Why do you think it is important?

Question: What is your favorite family tradition and why?

Question: If your family reserved one night a week for a family activity, what would you want it to be and why?

5. Dream Catcher (Web of Support)

Suggested Group Size: 8–16

Purpose: This exercise will help parents understand how important it is for their children to have multiple forms of support. If you have a larger group, build several webs at the same time.

Estimated Time: 12–15 minutes

Materials: One roll of crepe paper or yarn per group; 10 balloons per group (12–15 inches in diameter)

Directions:

1. Form groups of 8–12 and have them stand close together in a circle.

2. Give one person in each group one roll of crepe paper or yarn. Ask that person to describe one way he or she currently encourages the positive growth of a young person (in her or his role as a parent, guardian, relative, neighbor, mentor, coach, leader, or teacher). Holding on to the end of the crepe paper or yarn, the person should toss the roll to a second person at least two people away.

3. The second person now describes his or her positive role in the life of a young person. Holding on to the crepe paper, this person tosses the roll to a third person. Continue the process until everyone in the circle has participated. If using yarn, consider going around the circle one more time to create a denser, stronger web.

4. As group leader, comment positively on all the individual acts of asset building that work together to form a strong community web for children's successful development. Encourage the group to pull on the streamers to "tighten up" their web so that it becomes the best possible network for supporting their youth.

5. Toss 10 balloons into each web and have the group bounce them on top of the web for two minutes.

6. Call "time's up" at two minutes. Ask participants to tell you what it was like trying to keep the balloons from hitting the floor. What strategies did they try?

7. If some of the balloons are still atop the web when you call time, tell the group to pretend that anyone born in January, February, or March has done enough for young people (their "fair share") and can now discontinue doing any more caring efforts. Have them drop their part of the web. What happens to the remaining balloons on top of the web?

8. Have each circle drop their web and reconvene the group as a whole. Discuss the reflection questions below.

Reflection:

- What happened when some participants dropped out of the web after they had "done enough" for young people?

- What did the exercise illustrate about the power of individuals to effect positive change?

- What does it really take to create a strong web of support for all youth?

All of these exercises can be used at parent gatherings. But this isn't the only way to get parents engaged. When parents plan a fundraiser, picnic, carnival, or other event, think about ways you can use some time after the event to celebrate your parent volunteers and also give them a chance to socialize.

Recruiting and Managing Parent Volunteers

Teachers and schools often use an open house or back-to-school night to recruit volunteers for the myriad activities that support the life of the school. At these events parent organizations often recruit volunteers for schoolwide activities such as fundraisers, picnics, parties, and other annual events. Classroom teachers are usually recruiting parent volunteers for their child's classroom.

Typically, the classroom pitch includes a list of all the "jobs" you're looking for parents and guardians to take on. (Of course, you may also be trying to reach grandparents and other interested community members who attend the back-to-school event as well.) You may send parents a checklist so they can indicate which opportunities they're interested in, or circulate a sign-up sheet around the room. This process often occurs after presentations have been made and parent questions have been fielded—when parents are looking at their watches and thinking about getting home to check on homework or move their children toward bedtime. If parents do sign up, they may forget to write down what they signed up for, leaving it to you or the volunteer coordinator to contact them and remind them what they agreed to do.

How can you improve the process? It helps to step into parents' shoes for just a moment to understand where they're coming from. Parents have their own hopes and dreams for their children's achievement, and must juggle multiple, competing agendas at home and work in order to also participate in the important work of the school. Here are some of the realities of parents who hope to volunteer:

> *I'd heard a little about the other students from my child, and I was curious to meet some of their parents. I was glad you started with a short "icebreaker" activity so that we could introduce ourselves and get to know each other a bit. And the name tags really helped. I knew a few of the parents from last year, but I could not, for the life of me, remember their names!*

A NOTE ABOUT "FIT"

Parents with good intentions may sign up for a task that you or they soon realize is not a good fit. Identifying the problem early and having a conversation can prevent ongoing frustration on your part and theirs. Perhaps a father enthusiastically signed up to listen to students read for an hour every week, but he's had trouble getting to the school regularly or on time. Acknowledging that it doesn't seem to be working can be uncomfortable, but it doesn't have to be painful.

For example, you might say, "I appreciate your willingness to listen to students read, but it seems that other commitments are making it hard for you to get here during our reading period. Is there another time of day or type of task that would be a better fit for your schedule?" You might want to suggest one or two—it will give the parent a chance to save face and exit gracefully from a time commitment that doesn't really work.

I showed up for back-to-school night even though I had raced home from work to feed my family first. My kids were challenging tonight. They hadn't completed their homework, and I had to leave a sink full of dishes waiting for me when I got back. I probably looked a little distracted, and I was. But I also cared about getting my children off to a good start this school year, and I wanted to meet their teachers to get a sense of how this year is going to go.

I know teachers have a lot on their plates, and can really use some assistance, but I just can't get away from work during the school day. Are there other ways I can be involved? What's the most important thing I should be doing at home to support my child?

I can hardly believe my child is starting middle school! I'm not at all sure what to expect or what the school and teachers expect from me. It was good that the staff shared some developmental information about what this age group is like and told why the school thinks it's important for parents to stay connected with their kids. On some days it's easy to connect with my kids, but on other days they just drive me crazy! It would be comforting to hear that the school sees my children making progress and enjoys the people they're becoming.

Finding Qualified Volunteers

School systems usually have their own procedures in place for conducting background checks on parent and community volunteers. Boards of directors of community and after-school programs and church governing bodies may also have clearly established policies for handling background checks. These policies should be available in writing for all parent volunteers. It's important to communicate to parents of all youth that safety procedures are in place and information about volunteers' qualifications is available upon request.

Sometimes, community sports teams, faith communities, and after-school programs may need to create their own set of procedures to ensure that volunteer candidates are appropriate for their jobs. Checking reliable references is often a good way to start. It's important to spend time identifying guidelines and procedures that can be applied fairly to all adults involved in working with youth, regardless of the program type. While outside the scope of this handbook, you can develop, implement, and enforce "safe volunteer" policies.

Welcoming Volunteers

Try these tips for welcoming and encouraging potential volunteers:

Thank everyone who shows up. Acknowledge that you know they made a choice to be present, and let them know how much you appreciate it.

Talk a little about how volunteers help you do your best work with students, and how they supplement the instruction you provide.

Be concise but specific about what the various volunteer options involve:

I'm looking for parents who can commit to one hour a week during our reading time (8:30–9:15) to listen to a group of two or three students read aloud.

I run math games between 10:00 and 10:45 on Fridays and could use three parents to circulate between tables and help students if they get stuck. All the math games are simple and have printed instructions with them.

I'm looking for a parent or grandparent who would like to come in and play checkers with students sometime between 1:00 and 3:00 in the afternoons. I have several students who really need another caring adult and a chance to work toward a reward every week, and you could be that person!

Some middle school students are working on their organizational skills. I need a couple of parents during homeroom time on Mondays. I'd like to send students to meet with you in the library and get your assistance organizing their assignments into a three-ring binder so they can get the week off to a good start. Hopefully by the end of October they'll be able to tackle this on their own, and your work will be done.

We do a big unit on Africa during January. I am looking for two parents who could come in between 2:45 and 3:30 once or twice a week to meet with small groups as they get ready for their presentations. I'll have an outline of what they should include in their reports and some tips you can share with them about organizing a presentation and working with a group. I am also looking for one or two guest speakers who have been to Africa, so I'm grateful if you can pass along names or contact information.

We do a theater production in May. I need several parents to help with sewing or finding simple costumes and listening to pairs of students practice their lines. On the evening of the performance (May 18), I need two parents to provide and serve cookies and drinks for parents who attend the event.

I could use help with bulletin boards, copying handouts, assembling packets, and other administrative tasks. These are things a parent could do before or after school hours, or they could be done at home.

Parents can decide which activity they feel comfortable with and identify the options that fit their schedule. Some parents feel comfortable working with a group of students. Some will panic at the thought of helping with math but may be comfortable working with students on a reading assignment, or vice versa. You may have a parent who enjoys finding resources for you. Whether they pay for the resources or are willing to do the legwork to locate supplies for you, their help can save you time. See the "School Volunteer Sign-Up" handout on page 101.

The "Nuts and Bolts" of Scheduling

Managing your parent volunteers is an ongoing effort that pays off in parents who keep showing up and making constructive contributions to your program or classroom. There are some nuts-and-bolts details that, when handled well, can smooth the path for parent volunteers. For example, some teachers have found that publishing a monthly calendar of who is volunteering when and including that in their newsletter accomplishes three things: It reminds parents of their time commitments, it acknowledges their presence to the other parents, and it encourages other parents to volunteer.

Similarly, if parents volunteer on a regular basis, be sure to let them know about field trips, all-school concerts, or all-school testing dates that could interfere with their regularly scheduled session. Parent volunteers will feel frustrated if they show up for their regular commitment and find your class engaged in another activity or, worse, out of the building. Failing to notify parents sends the message that you don't value their time.

There are three keys to effective volunteer management:

- Help them feel competent.

- Help them feel visible.

- Help them feel they are making a difference.

Help Them Feel Competent

The first step is to equip volunteers with the tools and knowledge they need to be successful. This might mean that you designate a quiet corner in the classroom where students can read to them, or supply them with discussion questions to use after showing a film during youth group. But it also includes providing the training they need to do the job effectively.

If parents volunteer to work directly with youth, both you and they have an interest in making sure they know how best to help youth. For example, if parents will be listening to young students practice their reading skills, you might first take 3 to 5 minutes to outline the three key points you want them to listen for, and the two strategies you want them to use when correcting students. The goal is not to turn them into teachers, but rather to give them the basics so they're able to use their time effectively and have a positive effect on students' reading skills.

A mother who has volunteered to help students with reading skills in many classrooms had this to say: "I was lucky because the first time I volunteered to help with reading, the teacher explained why fluency was important and suggested I let minor mispronunciations go as long as it seemed they were getting most of the words right. She asked me to stop the student at the end of each paragraph or page and ask, 'So what was the key point in the section you just read?' If students could tell me what the section was about, I was to praise them briefly for getting it right and to keep going. If they couldn't get the main point, we went back and looked at the first sentence in each paragraph, to see if that told us what the key idea was going to be. Those were some simple but tangible suggestions, and I felt as though I was doing something useful for the student. She also had me work with the same two or three students for much of the school year. I really got to see their progress."

However, the mother continued, "Last year the teacher sent a different student out of the room with me every week. I'm supposed to listen to them read, but if I hadn't had that earlier training, I'd be pretty ineffective. I don't really know how any of the students are doing since I rarely saw the same one again, and that meant I couldn't really form a relationship with them either. That has to be uncomfortable for the student—reading to a stranger every time. I know it is for me."

Three parents were comparing notes about their volunteer experiences. One mother laughed and said, "The first day I showed up I was told to work with two students on their math assignment. The assignment was multiplying fractions. I haven't done that since I was in grade school. Luckily one of the students had a textbook with

ESTABLISHING AND MAINTAINING BOUNDARIES

Occasionally there are parent volunteers with whom you really "click." They are helpful, you share similar interests, and you enjoy each other's company. While this can be one of the fringe benefits of getting to know your volunteers, you also need to balance these friendships with the perceptions of others. Whether it's true or not, some parents may believe that your closeness to one parent over others also means that you favor that parent's child over the other students.

If you set personal boundaries for how you will behave toward volunteers, it's less likely that conflicts of interest will arise. For the volunteer system to run smoothly, all parents need to feel equally valued and comfortable approaching you with any questions or concerns. This becomes especially important if these concerns center around other volunteers—if you come across as partial to the volunteer in question, others may not want to discuss the problems with you. Issues between volunteers can result in volunteers quitting or being unsatisfied in their position. There is no hard-and-fast guideline about how friendly you should be, but pay attention to how you spend your time with parent volunteers and strive for some balance. If you're unsure about this, check in with another staff person to test your perceptions.

ACCEPTING LIMITATIONS

It can be overwhelming to find, train, and retain volunteers—as much as you need their help, sometimes accepting it feels like *more* work!

Remember that not only do you appreciate your volunteers, they appreciate you and the role you play in their child's life. You know you need to thank your volunteers for their time and that it's important that you make their jobs as easy and productive as possible, but sometimes details do slip through the cracks. So you barely had time to glance in the volunteer's direction yesterday—cut yourself some slack. You have to rein in the attention of 30 or more young people, and you have a lot to cover in the time you're together. Resolve to touch base with the volunteer next time.

One retired classroom teacher says that during her 50 years of teaching she had many classroom volunteers who helped her provide a strong program, and while she tried to acknowledge each volunteer each time, her primary focus was on teaching and keeping her students on task.

"If anyone got ignored or had to proceed without direct instruction it was the parent," she says.

Once the parent volunteers were trained, she expected them to work independently and save any questions that weren't urgent until the school day was over.

"Even during prep time I had other things to do," she says.

While it is important to thank parents present answer their questions with patience and grace, remind yourself that parent volunteers are there to help make your classroom or program as effective as possible, and not there to get a pat on the back.

What if you're a classroom teacher and you'd really rather not have parents present

cont'd

them and I peeked back in the section to figure out how they were supposed to be doing the problems. Without that book it would have been a wasted hour."

The second parent said, "I had to work with math problems, too. But the teacher gave me a little chart that had the basic processes and formulas written down so I could use that to help explain the problems to the students."

The third parent said, "I hated math in school and never really got it. I'm lucky I got to work with a student on spelling words. That, I understand. If I had to do math, I probably wouldn't come back."

Parents who feel ineffective may look for excuses not to return. This leaves you with fewer volunteers and students with fewer caring adults to give them extra help. A small amount of training or preparation can make a big difference in how volunteers feel about their time with you and the students.

Help Them Feel Visible

It is easy, once volunteer routines are established, to nod at parents as they come in and settle down to their assigned tasks, and to continue with what you were doing. It is important, though, to make a point of touching base with them during the time they are there. In addition to offering a smile as they enter and a thank-you as they leave, add an occasional "How's it going?" to be sure everything is on track. No one likes to feel invisible. And if they do feel invisible, then it's pretty easy to just disappear. That's not good for you and not good for them.

If you have volunteers who arrive after a lesson has started, then you might need to rethink arrival time to ensure you have a minute or two to chat and catch up before the lesson begins. Or perhaps every other week you can join volunteers for a quick cup of coffee and a chat at the end of their shift. Another option is to set up a regular coffee time before school on a set day of the week or month, so volunteers can ask questions and talk with each other about strategies they've used to help students with their work. Think of creative ways to acknowledge your parent volunteers. Perhaps students can write thank-you notes to classroom volunteers as part of a writing exercise, or create a colorful name tag for each of your parent volunteers. The acknowledgment can be simple, as long as it conveys the message, "We're glad you're here! Thanks for coming."

Help Them Feel They Are Making a Difference

Volunteers are present in your classroom for a relatively short period of time—weekly, monthly, or only occasionally. Often, parents may not be able to observe the change over time that you see in students' skills and knowledge acquisition or estimate the contribution they are making. While you need to preserve the confidentiality surrounding your students' progress, it *is* possible to let parent volunteers know that you see signs of progress in the students with whom they are working. You can tell parents the positive things students said about the party that volunteers helped orchestrate, or about the field trip they chaperoned. Letting parents know that their presence matters is one of the most effective ways to retain volunteers.

Teams, After-School Programs, and Faith Communities

Coordinating the many details that are part of community or after-school youth activities is no small feat. With a notebook, a phone list, and time set aside for calling, e-mailing, and talking to parents in person, you'll make a good head start on the process. In this section we look at the particular tasks of volunteer coordinators for sports teams, after-school programming, and faith community activities.

Regardless of the setting for your program, what often counts most with parents is the welcome and hospitality you show as the parent involvement coordinator. Any time you approach parents with graciousness and an understanding that they have positive qualities to contribute, you communicate clearly that you value their potential contribution and will be more likely to receive a "yes" response to your request. They will remember you the next time they are asked.

Keep records of parents you ask, when you ask them, and for what position, as well as the reasons parents decline an invitation (if that's the case). This allows you to more strategically target them in the future for jobs tailored to their situation. (See handout "Volunteer Here!" on page 102.) Remember, the goal is to engage *every* parent. And all parents can be given a sense that they belong comfortably somewhere within a youth-focused organization, just as every child can be given the assurance that he belongs and makes a positive contribution.

Parents want to be asked and have the same need to belong and feel valued as the kids in your program. You can impart this sense of belonging to potential volunteers by learning their names and their children's names. Sometimes parents comment that they haven't volunteered recently (or ever) because they felt they were just another warm body being asked to fill a slot, not a person who was recognized

while you teach their children? That's okay—there are plenty of other ways you can use parents' skills and willingness to help.

"Some teachers do not encourage parent volunteers in the classroom because the teacher can't avoid the adult interaction with the parent," says the retired teacher. "Student behavior can be off task quickly when the teacher is otherwise engaged."

She says that some parents need adult interaction and use their time in the classroom to obtain it. Teacher-volunteer relationships can become awkward when parents overstep their bounds and try to socialize with the teacher, to the detriment of an appropriate learning environment for the children.

"It takes experience, self-confidence, and clear vision to deal with this situation."

Whether it's hockey or Little League baseball, one dad is out there coaching every year. He played sports when he was young and loves working with the kids. He'll be hard to replace when his kids finally age out of those programs.

and known. Or perhaps they weren't sure they had time, or felt unappreciated for past efforts. Sometimes parents can't cope with the unpredictability of a task, or feel shy around parents they do not know. When you can address these concerns, you will remove barriers to participation. Try these tips for laying the groundwork and increasing the likelihood you'll get a potential volunteer to say yes:

Use "bleacher time" to make introductions between people who haven't met before, and circulate among parents every time you're in their presence (rather than sitting only with your own friends or racing out of religious services without stopping to introduce yourself and greet newcomers).

Draw in parents who are clearly new to a setting by introducing yourself and your family and asking about their family. Be sure to write down their names and contact information right away. If families are new to your area (and perhaps to this country) you will gain a reputation as a skilled diplomat and master volunteer coordinator if you take the extra time to speak clearly, listen to their cultural concerns, and help them make connections with strategic community groups and resource people, if needed.

Find volunteer jobs that can be done by parents with small children (such as stuffing envelopes, making calls, or providing treats for the team), or offer childcare in a safe setting to free parents to volunteer on behalf of their child who is enrolled in your program.

Always be sure to express thanks to parents for a job well done! A gratified parent is likely to volunteer again.

Tips for Sports Team Parent Volunteers

A few key rules apply to volunteers who are parents of young people involved in sports teams. First, communicate to parent volunteers that their teamwork is just as vital to the success of the team sport as their children's own efforts. Parents are sometimes inclined to impose their own ambitions, thwarted or otherwise, onto their children's sporting efforts. One good way to draw their attention away from this behavior is to emphasize that volunteering (however imperfect it may be), is about working toward one's personal best (just as is participating in the sport for the young person). See the handout "The Parents' Good Sport Code of Conduct" on page 106.

Support your sporting parent volunteers just as you want them to provide moral support to their own athletes. Don't overcoach your volunteers; allow them to do their volunteer jobs in the best way they can without micromanaging the process. Pay compliments and make positive remarks to your volunteers in the same way that you would want coaches to compliment their children's efforts.

Be sure to check in with volunteers to ask whether they are uncomfortable with any aspect of their volunteer job after they've gotten started. Often, small adjustments can be made to a volunteer's task that greatly increases their comfort and satisfaction and increases their likelihood of success and future participation.

Tips for Faith Community Parent Volunteers

Parent support and involvement is as critical to the successful education of children involved in faith-formation programs as it is in secular settings. In fact, with the guidance and leadership of trained clergy and lay leaders, parents often make up the backbone of congregational education efforts. Experienced parent volunteer coordinators in faith-based community settings emphasize the importance of establishing regular, comprehensive communication with parents of children involved in a faith community's classes and programs.

Marian Clark, a longtime parent volunteer coordinator for a Minnesota faith community, uses a variety of strategies that keep parents informed about their children's religious education and actively involved in helping provide that education. Clark suggests the following tips:

Create a calendar for families that anticipates as many major events, registration dates, and program deadlines as possible. Give the calendar to parents several times. Send it to parents a month in advance of the start of the program season, along with registration materials. Make extra copies available at a sign-up table before and after religious services. Hand the calendar to parents at an organizational parent meeting that kicks off the new program year. Use e-mail and your faith community's Web site to post dates and key details of youth education programs, mission-related trips, and religious activities. Using various modes of delivery helps parents gradually assimilate information that would otherwise overwhelm and confuse them, or get lost or never arrive if offered only once.

Keep two contact lists of parents and children—one for snail mail and one for e-mail. Use the regular mail list for communications that all parents need to receive, including information about curriculum plans, expectations for children's participation and behavior, newsletters, special event information, and parent surveys. Create a second list that consists of parents' e-mail addresses and use it to send timely reminders and requests several days to weeks in advance of key events. E-mail can function as an overlapping mail path, but it's also important to provide parents with important information on paper, as neither method is completely guaranteed to reach the intended reader.

Use your faith community's weekly bulletin or order of service to announce information parents need to see about children's classes and activities, in addition to the communications techniques mentioned above.

Take advantage of speaking time during services to repeat important information, remind parents of upcoming events, and ask for volunteer help.

Create a parent newsletter that offers specific updates to information you provided at the beginning of the year. Send it home quarterly or periodically. Know your community and its individual characteristics. Offer separate sections that address concerns voiced by parents of children in specific segments or age-bands in your program (by grade, age, or advancement level). Provide parents with tips about faith formation that are developmentally based. A question-and-answer format incorporating the typical questions parents may have or that children may ask them works well for this purpose.

A newsletter can also be an appropriate place to offer parents an "emergency kit" of information that addresses the faith community's views on significant issues that children and teenagers grapple with. You can provide parents with specific contacts within your community for special care, advice, or assistance with sensitive topics. In times of crisis, your newsletter can be a trusted source of information that parents can turn to with confidence.

You don't necessarily have to write new material from scratch if it already exists as an electronic link on your faith community's local or national Web site. It's appropriate to say to parents, "For more information on these questions or topics, see the following link . . . " If your faith community includes speakers of multiple languages, offer a variety of Web links in those languages.

Avoid "information overload" by sending information to parents when they are ready for it and really need it. Learn to anticipate these times, and send parents information slightly ahead of the expected need. You can offer parents a preview of faith-based rituals and teachings that their children will be introduced to over time. These are the "transition times" or "big times" in a faith-based program when children move from one stage to the next; for instance, when they become eligible to participate in a particular religious rite or ceremony, when they are transitioning from childhood to adulthood in the eyes of the congregation, or when they are "graduating" from a particular phase in their religious life. Provide links to the Web sites of respected experts in your community to supplement communications.

Parents want to know where to go for information when they and their children are ready for it. Pay attention to the ebb and flow of their information needs. Offering parents pertinent information in an organized framework helps them persevere in their commitment to accompanying children through the process of faith education. Having complete information also helps parents establish a predictable routine that young people can depend upon.

Use the 10 minutes before or after youth classes or meetings to hold parent update meetings. Consider serving drinks and light snacks and providing a quick hands-on activity for young people while you meet with their parents. Clark suggests that youth attendance at all functions will increase and be more consistent when you regularly and frequently communicate with parents in these brief "before and after" parent meetings.

Hold a family dinner gathering (before afternoon or evening youth programs) that doubles as a parent meeting, and you'll attract more participants. Presenting a simple, nutritious meal for parents and children will draw greater numbers of participants across all settings, not just in faith-based communities. Use the time while people are eating to make announcements. You'll accomplish several goals at once: encourage families to build community relationships and strengthen their own family ties, communicate key information to parents, and ensure that participants are well fed and ready to participate fully in your programming.

When Classroom Volunteers Struggle with a Task

Sometimes teachers find that interactions between parent volunteers and a group of children are not working. Your first job is to assess the specific issue.

Are parents leaping in to do students' work for them? Offer parents a short coaching session with a list that identifies the activities you expect children to complete. Suggest strategies volunteers can use to guide the children through the task. Let parents know that part of the expected outcome is for students to learn from the process of working together as a group, identifying and correcting their own mistakes as they go.

Do parents correct every mispronounced word as children read new material aloud? Share tutoring strategies that help students gain reading fluency while encouraging them to take risks with their guesses about how words sound. Offer tips on how to work with reluctant readers. Skills that volunteers develop while working with students in your classroom will also make them more effective teachers with their own children at home.

Do parent volunteers feel uncomfortable with the subject matter? The way you teach math concepts, for example, may be very different from the way parents learned the same concepts when they were in school. A set of formulas or a brief summary that outlines the step-by-step process you teach to students will give parents confidence and help them be more successful in their tutoring. If coaching and tip sheets don't seem to help, suggest another academic subject or project that parents feel comfortable with.

Remember that just as students want to be successful, so do parents. Appropriate preparation, discreet coaching, and timely feedback along the way can help parents do their best as they assist you in the classroom.

Empowering Parents to Be Successful Leaders

A critical element of parent engagement is inviting all parents into authentic decision-making processes. Regardless of skill levels, economic circumstances, and other personal characteristics, parents will support and trust you when you acknowledge their hopes and concerns for their children's educations and encourage them to join in groups and actions that make decisions benefiting their children.

With encouragement, parents often make substantial contributions of time and effort on behalf of their children's education. They learn to work with—not against—teachers and leaders of their children. They form relationships with other parents and staff members. They feel actively involved in helping their children achieve success. And they become a part of something larger than themselves.

What do those decision-making processes look like? Opportunities for parents to actively influence decisions that affect their children's education and after-school activities include participating in school and community focus groups, sitting on No Child Left Behind (NCLB)–mandated parent advisory committees, joining after-school and faith-based activity leadership teams and athletic boards of directors, and taking active roles in parent-teacher organization meetings.

Other important decision-making roles in which parents can influence education policy outcomes include advocacy efforts (writing letters to legislators and lobbying elected representatives to improve learning conditions for all children); participating in telephone, e-mail, paper, and in-person surveys that give direction to administrators and teachers; offering informed comments and views at local school board meetings; and fundraising for causes related to children's education and extracurricular activities.

Parents and school staff can find common ground and shared wisdom by participating in one-time or occasional book groups that focus on education issues. Parents can organize and participate in school- or community-wide culture clubs that bring together families from different racial and ethnic backgrounds. They can also partner with the teachers and staff of their children's schools and after-school programs to build community relationships through service projects. All these actions allow parents to be known, heard, and valued.

Specific parental decision-making roles are explored in the following sections, along with suggestions for encouraging parents to take leadership roles in their children's education and extracurricular activities.

Parent Speakers

Often, parents are willing, able, and excited to make classroom or group presentations on a variety of topics related to your curriculum or program goals. You can accomplish several aims at once through your strategic use of parent speakers. Tapping parents' unique experience and knowledge base deepens children's classroom learning, allows parents of various backgrounds to share their cultures and promote a positive understanding of differences, offers parents a chance to see their children interact with peers and adults in a different context, and helps parents feel a sense of partnership with and appreciation for their children's teachers and activity leaders.

Using the list of volunteers you've gathered from sign-up sheets, conversations with parents, and other referrals, plan your schedule to include occasional parent presentations at key points in the school or program year. For tips on presenting material that captures kids' attention in classroom and group settings, give parents the handout "Success Tips for Classroom Presenters" on page 108. Emphasize the power of storytelling, rather than lecturing, and encourage speakers to make their presentations interactive with props, audio recordings, and other sensory experiences.

For parents who may not be familiar with written English, take time to speak to them directly before their presentation or demonstration so that you can summarize the points contained in this handout.

Legislative Action

Help parents create persuasive mail campaigns that attract the attention of elected representatives by giving them "Writing Your Legislators: Advocacy Tips for Parents" and "Sample Legislative Action Letters" on pages 110 and 111–112. These handouts offer writers concrete strategies for clearly expressing their thoughts in brief, direct, informed language. The handouts suggest a number of ways to incorporate parents' personal experiences and anecdotes in their letters.

Some parents may also be able to lobby elected officials through courteous phone calls, face-to-face meetings, and attendance at large group meetings. Recommend that parents familiarize themselves as much as possible with the issues and with the job descriptions of the officials they plan to contact to maximize their effectiveness. Parents can do this by carefully reading legislative Web sites or other literature that explains the decision-making scope of the people with whom they will be in touch. It is important for parents to respect a legislator's time and know the responsibilities and limits of a legislator's positions and ability to effect change.

Community Service Partnerships

When parents, children, and community partners come together in service partnerships, the abstract notion of "working for the common good" becomes a meaningful reality. Kate Olson, volunteer coordinator and food shelf manager of the St. Louis Park Emergency Program (STEP) of St. Louis Park, Minnesota, says that she has had great success piloting a program that involves families in volunteer work for the food shelf. She gathers an e-mail list of individuals and families in the community who want to be notified of upcoming early evening and weekend volunteer openings, and sends a monthly e-mail listing the days and times she needs help. The one-and-a-half-hour shifts can be done on a one-time-only or recurring basis. The program invites parents to bring children of all ages, but makes it clear that families with small children can leave after one hour if young children's attention spans don't allow them to stay engaged.

"It's a wonderful way to stay connected with volunteer opportunities for the family, but is also flexible enough so that it's doable for families that have a tight schedule with kids' activities and work and such," Olson says. "It's been so exciting to see families volunteering together and being engaged in the local services in their community."

To set up a volunteer opportunities mailing, collect parent e-mail addresses from your beginning-of-the-season sign-up sheets and compile them into a group format. Be sure to give the group a name such as "Volunteer Opportunities Listing" in your e-mail address book and place all e-mail addresses in the blind carbon copy (BCC) section so that they do not show in the header of the e-mail when you send out requests for volunteers. Create a list of short-term opportunities for service by families and individuals in your school or program and update it periodically. When you send a monthly mailing to volunteers, consider communicating it in three separate formats to reach the widest possible audience. For instance, you can get the word out using paper newsletters or postcards, voice-mail recordings, and your organization's Web site, in addition to e-mail.

Fundraising

Fundraising is a given in many schools, community youth programs, faith community settings, and sports and after-school activities. Setting and meeting the budget for your needs requires a team of honest, conscientious, and careful individuals who can successfully execute a fundraising plan. In more and more cash-strapped school systems, parents are even creating nonprofit foundations whose sole purpose is to raise money to supplement the budget and support the mission of the public schools.

Whether your goal is to raise money for a single purpose, such as a scoreboard or a mission trip, or to create an ongoing source of funding to supplement teacher salaries or critical arts initiatives, be sure to establish logical procedures for communicating with parent volunteers, handling money, and meeting reporting and accounting requirements.

Create a set of fundraising policies and procedures and make sure all volunteers receive and understand them. A carefully chosen fundraising coordinator should convene a meeting for this purpose.

Organize a logical chain of regular contacts between the school or program, volunteer fundraisers, and the families involved in the organization.

Set up a checking or savings account that requires two signatures for withdrawals.

Make sure volunteer fundraisers understand how to account for any funds they collect. It's always best to have a minimum of two adults held accountable for handling money.

Use a school safe or your program's lockbox for funds that are in transit to the bank. Deposits should be made promptly by a school official or designated treasurer who has the authority to handle money and follows procedures for safekeeping.

Keep all parents in the communication loop about your fundraising purposes, goals, and progress by sending frequent, predictable updates. Make it clear how much money is raised and how much will be spent by publicizing a brief budget summary.

Give parents involved in fundraisers for your school or program the handout "Sample Fundraising Letter" (on page 108) on which they can model their initial contacts with identified companies or individuals.

Volunteers can mail or hand-deliver the letter to potential funders. It is a good idea to call funding prospects in advance to establish who has the authority to disburse funds. Use school or program letterhead stationery. Include the person's mailing address and the date in business letter format.

Culture Clubs and Parent Book Groups

More recent forms of parent engagement in schools involve culture clubs and parent book groups that are jointly led by parents, teachers, and staff. Culture clubs may include book readings, but are generally broader in scope and are an ideal way to reach out to families who are new to the country or who are learning English (but all families are welcomed). Families meet for a meal and share their food and customs, including music, dance, art, and crafts, with each other. Programming often focuses on one country or culture per meeting, and is an ideal way to promote intercultural understanding among various ages, grades, ethnicities, and religious groups. Newcomers frequently make connections and begin to feel less "outside the system" as a result of celebrating their cultural diversity.

Parent book club members meet to discuss articles and books that address important cultural and academic themes that affect their children and schools or programs. One young mother of elementary school children in Minneapolis had this to say about her school's book club:

> One of the teachers in our school decided to invite any parents
> and teachers interested in reading and discussing The Middle
> of Everywhere: The World's Refugees Come to Our Town
> by Mary Pipher [2002] to form a book club that would meet
> after school. We had great discussions, and I learned about
> the efforts being made by teachers to connect with newcomer
> children and their parents in our community. The book club
> opened my eyes to the situations of families right here—trying
> to speak a new language, learning about how things work in
> our school, and figuring out all the cultural references that
> seemed so strange to them.

Book clubs can be a vehicle for honest discussions of differences in a safe and respectful atmosphere. Titles that parents and staff may

ADVOCATING FOR CHANGE

Jeff Syme and Terry Gunderson are involved parents of two girls, an 8th grader and a 5th grader. Terry has served on a principal selection committee, and Jeff is currently the chair of the site council at his youngest daughter's school.

"We both volunteer for field trips and school visits, and attend virtually every school function," Jeff says. "There are many other hands-on parents like us—and there are many more hands-off parents who you never see at school, of course."

Recently, the school district's vote on an important issue shocked Terry and Jeff, as well as other parents.

"[It] caught everyone by surprise and caused a huge amount of turmoil in the two weeks preceding the vote," he says. "We formed a quick group, and one parent created a Web site to coordinate our thoughts and energies."

Jeff and Terry couldn't just sit back and let the decision go unnoticed. Along with other concerned parents, they have resolved to make the best out of a bad situation—"the old lemonade out of lemons thing," he says—and continue to seek facts and information, get families and other stakeholders involved, meet with school representatives, and contact their legislators.

Jeff's advice to parents with schoolchildren is to get involved and stay involved.

"Like almost everything in life, you get out of it what you put into it—and Terry and I both have a very high commitment to our kids and to their education. We know they are doing their part at school, and we want to support them and all their friends and their classmates as well."

Jeff and Terry participate in school matters not only for their own children, but for the benefit of all students, including those who

cont'd

find enlightening include *The Spirit Catches You and You Fall Down: A Hmong Child, Her American Doctors, and the Collision of Two Cultures* (1998) by Anne Fadiman; *White Teacher* (2000) by Vivian Gussin Paley; *Unfinished Business: Closing the Racial Achievement Gap in Our Schools* (2006) by Pedro Noguera and Jean Yonemura Wing; and *Other People's Children: Cultural Conflict in the Classroom* (1996) by Lisa Delpit.

Surveys and Focus Groups

An effective way to bring parents into decision-making roles and leadership positions in your school is to invite them to participate in surveys and focus groups. Surveys can be given to parents in person or on paper at parent-teacher organization meetings, open houses, parent conferences, and through e-mail and regular mail. The importance of surveys is that they offer a way for parents to provide direct and honest commentary about issues that affect their children and their families. Construct your survey to cover the big issues, as well as leaving room for open-ended responses. Don't make it too long, however, or you will lose your audience (no more than two pages is best). Be sure to collate responses and publicize the results, using them as the basis for thoughtful action in your program.

Focus groups are ideal vehicles for learning more from parents about their children's and their own direct experiences with your curriculum or programming. Groups of 8–10 parents led by a trained focus group leader (another parent or staff member) can offer helpful insights into what's going well and what needs work in your setting. Lead the focus group through a prepared set of questions. Be respectful of participants' time by limiting the discussion to about 45 minutes. To capture the widest possible group of participants, offer several focus group meetings at various times of the day and week. Focus groups can be prime opportunities to invite underrepresented members of your community to participate and add their voice to your planning processes. Be sure to offer light refreshments and take time to make introductions and get to know members of the group.

Committees and Boards of Directors

Other forms of parent involvement extend to membership and leadership on academic and advisory committees, councils, and boards of directors. These are important roles for parents to take on. But instead of always appointing the same vocal parents each time to these roles, consider seeking the widest possible representation by appointing quiet parents who may need encouragement to speak their minds, or parents who are marginalized for a variety of reasons (for instance, their economic, ethnic, education, or religious status). It is vital that parents from all walks of life be given a voice, and that all other parents hear that voice.

A key requirement of the No Child Left Behind (NCLB) mandate is that parents must now be engaged by all school systems in some form of advisory group representation. Parent members of curriculum advisory committees can serve as spokespersons for the committee when they return to their parent and family groups within the community and the school.

Parent-Teacher Organizations

Parent-teacher organizations are a critical vehicle for cultivating engaged parents in schools. They offer parents a way to become involved in every aspect of school life as it affects their children. Parents form effective working relationships with teachers, principals, and other staff, and gain a better understanding of the challenges that teaching professionals face every day. Staff members get to know parents better and gain respect for parents' experiences, concerns, and abilities.

To maximize parent interest and involvement, offer flexible meeting times (one school offered dual groups, which met monthly both during the lunch hour and in the early evening). Be sure to actively promote meetings in your school newsletters, e-mails, and on your Web site. Serve light refreshments, and feature useful topics that meet a need parents have (topics relating to children's development, such as growing independence, the onset of puberty, planning for college and work, and dealing with troubling behaviors). If the topic is relevant and the speaker is engaging and reputable, parents will be much more likely to come. Offer childcare and translators, if at all possible.

The parent-teacher organization can be a key structure for cultivating parent leadership in roles such as fundraising; acting as liaisons to academic committees; assisting with creating communications such as schoolwide directories, parent handbooks, and newsletters; serving as classroom representatives and bridges between teachers, students, and other parents; and becoming active in advocating for education policy changes at the local, state, and national levels. The National Parent Teacher Association offers an extensive array of well-written resources for parent involvement at its Web site, www.pta.org.

will attend the district's schools in the future. They believe that if parents want changes in their child's education, they cannot sit back and wait for the changes to happen.

"There's no substitution for digging in and doing the work, or helping do the work, to get the results you want," Jeff says.

Appreciating and Celebrating Parent Involvement

After recruiting, interacting with, and managing many volunteers—parents and guardians, extended family members, and others—throughout the program year, it's appropriate to express genuine appreciation to them for their time, effort, talent, and caring guidance. Certainly, the students and youth in your program are the direct beneficiaries of all that nurturing attention, and now it's time to be sure your volunteers know it.

At the most fundamental level, an authentic "thank you" is appreciated by everyone. These words never go out of style. A simple thank-you can make a profound impact on a person's ongoing commitment to the project or effort. Resolve to thank your volunteers at the end of each volunteer session and couple your thanks with a specific statement that reflects your understanding of the volunteer's effort:

> *Thank you for listening to Elizabeth read this morning—her mother has a new baby at home and hasn't had much time to spend with her in the last few weeks. Did you notice how she warmed up to you as you listened to her and helped her sound out new words?*

> *Devon was really out of sorts this morning until you arrived to work with him on his math problems. You have a knack for helping him calm down, focus, and trust his own instincts for solving tough problems. Thank you!*

It's crucial not to take for granted the value of volunteers' time. When teachers, coaches, youth workers, religious leaders, and volunteer coordinators demonstrate an understanding of the choices and sacrifices volunteers make to participate in a project, volunteers leave feeling good about themselves and the work they're doing.

Thanking others does require your *own* time, effort, and thoughtfulness, but it is well worth the investment—it results in renewed volunteer vigor, encourages volunteers to spread positive assessments of the work they're doing, and enhances the reputation of the program in the community. When volunteerism "catches on" as something others want to be part of, you'll know it. Here's the story of one classroom volunteer who came to a teacher's aid in a pinch:

I received a completely unexpected and lovely thank-you note from my daughter's social studies teacher one summer after I helped her out in a jam. She had called me at the last minute, not knowing who else to turn to, because she needed someone to give two of her students rides to their summer activity program when she became ill. The girls were from families that did not own cars, and they would not otherwise have been able to participate in their mock trial and debate program. I just happened to be free that day, and the girls were so thankful for the ride. It made me feel so good to do something simple yet meaningful for them. It also helped me appreciate how transportation can be such a barrier to participation for some families. I was glad the teacher had thought to call me, and I was suddenly made aware of the depth of this teacher's commitment to the well-being of her students.

Going Beyond "Thank You"

Recognizing the efforts of volunteers starts with verbal thank-yous. If time allows, it's important to go beyond that level of acknowledgment when volunteer contributions are significant. Students and young people will grasp the importance of gratitude when you model it in the classroom or within your program, because they naturally observe the behaviors modeled by their leader (you). They do make the connection between efforts of volunteers on their behalf and the appropriate thanks that are offered in exchange.

Periodically offer additional forms of thanks to your volunteers, using the following suggestions as starting points:

Have students or young people in your program write thank-you notes to volunteers on personal notepaper or hand-drawn cards. Hewlett-Packard's Web site offers free thank-you card designs at www.hp.com/go/activity center. A variety of attractive ethnic designs are featured.

Ask young students to decorate white business-length envelopes, which can be stored and used later as mailing envelopes for thank-you notes written throughout the school year.

Create certificates that can be customized to reflect the personalities of students or program participants.

Direct students to create art that reflects the specific activity the volunteer took part in.

Organize a volunteer recognition ceremony and serve cake or other celebratory food that captures the spirit of the volunteer assignment.

Designate special community volunteer appreciation days (through civic proclamations or schoolwide volunteer event days).

Provide volunteers with coupons for free food or discounts at local businesses.

Hold an end-of-the-season volunteer luncheon or dinner. Tell brief (one- to two-sentence) verbal anecdotes about the contributions of each volunteer.

Collect spare change from students or young people in your program and use it to make a donation (as your budget allows) in the names of your volunteers.

Make a noncash contribution that honors volunteers' work. For example, plant a tree, establish a rain or rock garden, designate a hallway or name a special room, building, or outdoor site in honor of volunteers, or purchase a class or school library book that bears a special bookplate.

Establish an "honor roll" of volunteers that you place on permanent display. Note the volunteers' names, roles, dates, and hours donated to the project. Update it regularly.

Inscribe volunteers' names on a plaque, publish them in a regular organizational newsletter, and print volunteer names on a banner that you hang in a prominent location.

Create a special pin or permanent name tag that designates the significance of the volunteers' contributions. For example, twist ribbons in the colors of the organization into a loop that you attach to a pin backing and write or use colored glue to personalize a tribute to volunteers.

Media-Savvy Volunteer Thank-Yous

In addition to the ideas mentioned above, effective written ways to demonstrate the value you place on your volunteers' work are public acknowledgments which are equally important in building social captal with volunteers and publicizing your programs. Consider the following:

- School and community newsletter tributes.
- Well-written group e-mail communications.

- Newspaper feature stories and letters of praise that appear in the "Letters to the Editor."

- Brief flyers of thanks to volunteers inserted into local utility bill mailings.

- Public words of recognition printed on a paper program and offered verbally by the head of the program (principal, head coach, program coordinator) in a formal setting (taking care to mention all names, even when some are not able to be present).

A Volunteer Recognition Event

Resolve to "do it right" in a well-organized volunteer recognition event that publicizes to the community how wonderful your volunteers are. When you can thank a large number of people at one time in the context of a formal event, you can maximize your message of thanks, reinforce the importance of the good work being done, and cultivate a spirit of ongoing commitment on the part of your volunteers. Be sure to acknowledge the contribution of each individual to the successes you see in the group over time. Here are tips for making a recognition event one that will be remembered fondly:

Compile a complete list of invitees' names and contact information. Use your volunteer check-in notebook to cull names for the list, but also review the names of all the young people in your program to jog your memory of other parent volunteers whose names may be missing. Note next to each name the volunteer job (or jobs) the person has carried out and the significance of the contribution.

Decide upon a budget for the event (from no-cost/no-frills to low-cost/potluck to a moderate outlay figured on a per-person basis). It is not necessary to spend much on a recognition ceremony; what will be remembered most is the sincerity and planning that is part of the gesture.

Choose a time and place that coincides with the natural end of a school or program year. If you hold a volunteer tea or coffee event during school or program hours, you'll likely draw volunteers who do not work outside the home, unless volunteers are able to leave their workplace over their lunch break. An evening event may draw more volunteers. You may decide to hold two events—one during the day and one in the evening—to maximize participation. If at all possible, provide childcare for young children in a safe setting to allow busy parents the best chance of participating in your recognition event.

Send volunteers invitations made by young people. Be sure to include an RSVP telephone number and e-mail address. Follow up with direct contact (e-mail, in person, or phone calls), and keep track of responses. It is often the follow-up contact that signals your commitment to the importance of the event. Volunteers may be more likely to attend after receiving your call.

Invite administrators, curriculum specialists, school board members, and local media representatives to attend your recognition event. Some may be willing to speak about the value of volunteerism and its impact on youth and school achievement, the community, and solid school and business ties. In this way, you can add an additional layer of significance and worth to parents' efforts.

Offer food as part of the event if your budget allows (this often succeeds in attracting volunteers and their families). It doesn't have to be elaborate: coffee, tea, milk, and juice with cookies or fruit are always appreciated. But it is possible to pull off a simple meal as well, particularly if you know the number of people planning to attend. If you are holding a school volunteer recognition event, contact your school's food service to see whether it can provide food at school rates or bake sheet cakes in the school kitchen for the event. A bakery or restaurant in your community may be willing to donate food or cater the event.

Ask students or youth involved in the program to serve drinks or food and act as hosts and greeters for the guests.

Prepare brief anecdotes that illustrate the impacts volunteers have had on particular students or groups of students. You can keep children's names anonymous, if that seems important.

Create and present certificates of thanks, special pins, or T-shirts that note volunteers' specific contributions or the number of hours they contributed to school or group success. If you have a central notebook for tracking volunteer time, this should be a straightforward task. (See the handout "Parents Are the Best!" on page 117 for a sample certificate.)

The Bottom Line

Appreciating and celebrating parents' efforts to actively engage with their children's learning often motivates parents to stay involved, continue the hard work of nurturing and guiding, and even try new ways of working with their kids. Parenting—that all-important yet elusive job with no fixed guidelines or performance reviews—becomes clearer and more manageable when parents receive encouraging feedback and support from teachers, youth leaders, coaches, and other parents and adults active in their children's lives. If parents know they're on the right track and that helping kids achieve and learn can be the result of a satisfying, collaborative partnership with teachers and other adults, they can rise to the challenge of raising and shaping young people to meet their highest potential.

When you help parents become fully engaged in their children's lives, you are doing important work. It comes down to clarifying your goals, and communicating them clearly, consistently, and persuasively. It also means that you look for every opportunity to build genuine and lasting relationships with the parents of children in your classroom or program. It means that you look for ways to encourage and nurture parents' efforts in your one-on-one meetings with them, as well as in group gatherings. It means that you intentionally look for openings to introduce and connect parents to each other to help them feel that they belong and are known. Involving parents in children's school and extracurricular lives also depends on successfully recruiting them as volunteers in various support roles, and on trusting parents enough to partner with you in leadership and decision-making roles within school and community settings. This is hard work, and the many barriers to participation are significant. But with careful planning, using the creative strategies outlined in this book, and armed with an optimistic outlook that parents do want the best for their children, you can use the skills and talents all parents possess so that you *engage every parent!*

HANDOUTS

Chapter 5: Icebreakers for Group Gatherings

Chapter 6: Recruiting and Managing Parent Volunteers

Chapter 7: Empowering Parents to Be Successful Leaders

Chapter 8: Appreciating and Celebrating Parent Involvement

40 DEVELOPMENTAL ASSETS FOR ADOLESCENTS (AGES 12–18)

Search Institute® has identified the following building blocks of healthy development—known as Developmental Assets®—that help young people grow up healthy, caring, and responsible.

EXTERNAL ASSETS

Support

1. **Family Support:** Family life provides high levels of love and support.
2. **Positive Family Communication:** Young person and her or his parent(s) communicate positively, and young person is willing to seek advice and counsel from parent(s).
3. **Other Adult Relationships:** Young person receives support from three or more nonparent adults.
4. **Caring Neighborhood:** Young person experiences caring neighbors.
5. **Caring School Climate:** School provides a caring, encouraging environment.
6. **Parent Involvement in Schooling:** Parent(s) are actively involved in helping young person succeed in school.

Empowerment

7. **Community Values Youth:** Young person perceives that adults in the community value youth.
8. **Youth as Resources:** Young people are given useful roles in the community.
9. **Service to Others:** Young person serves in the community one hour or more per week.
10. **Safety:** Young person feels safe at home, at school, and in the neighborhood.

Boundaries and Expectations

11. **Family Boundaries:** Family has clear rules and consequences, and monitors the young person's whereabouts.
12. **School Boundaries:** School provides clear rules and consequences.
13. **Neighborhood Boundaries:** Neighbors take responsibility for monitoring young people's behavior.
14. **Adult Role Models:** Parent(s) and other adults model positive, responsible behavior.
15. **Positive Peer Influence:** Young person's best friends model responsible behavior.
16. **High Expectations:** Both parent(s) and teachers encourage the young person to do well.

Constructive Use of Time

17. **Creative Activities:** Young person spends three or more hours per week in lessons or practice in music, theater, or other arts.
18. **Youth Programs:** Young person spends three or more hours per week in sports, clubs, or organizations at school and/or in community organizations.
19. **Religious Community:** Young person spends one hour or more per week in activities in a religious institution.
20. **Time at Home:** Young person is out with friends "with nothing special to do" two or fewer nights per week.

INTERNAL ASSETS

Commitment to Learning

21. **Achievement Motivation:** Young person is motivated to do well in school.

22. **School Engagement:** Young person is actively engaged in learning.

23. **Homework:** Young person reports doing at least one hour of homework every school day.

24. **Bonding to School:** Young person cares about her or his school.

25. **Reading for Pleasure:** Young person reads for pleasure three or more hours per week.

Positive Values

26. **Caring:** Young person places high value on helping other people.

27. **Equality and Social Justice:** Young person places high value on promoting equality and reducing hunger and poverty.

28. **Integrity:** Young person acts on convictions and stands up for her or his beliefs.

29. **Honesty:** Young person "tells the truth even when it is not easy."

30. **Responsibility:** Young person accepts and takes personal responsibility.

31. **Restraint:** Young person believes it is important not to be sexually active or to use alcohol or other drugs.

Social Competencies

32. **Planning and Decision Making:** Young person knows how to plan ahead and make choices.

33. **Interpersonal Competence:** Young person has empathy, sensitivity, and friendship skills.

34. **Cultural Competence:** Young person has knowledge of and comfort with people of different cultural/racial/ethnic backgrounds.

35. **Resistance Skills:** Young person can resist negative peer pressure and dangerous situations.

36. **Peaceful Conflict Resolution:** Young person seeks to resolve conflict nonviolently.

Positive Identity

37. **Personal Power:** Young person feels he or she has control over "things that happen to me."

38. **Self-Esteem:** Young person reports having a high self-esteem.

39. **Sense of Purpose:** Young person reports that "my life has a purpose."

40. **Positive View of Personal Future:** Young person is optimistic about her or his personal future.

GOAL SETTING: WHAT DO YOU NEED FROM PARENTS AND FAMILIES?

Identify Your Goals for Parent Involvement

	MY GOALS AND STRATEGIES	HOW PARENTS CAN HELP
Clear Two-Way Communication with Children and Parents		
Homework or Practice		
Parent Volunteers		
Desired Outcomes		
Other Goals		

GETTING ORGANIZED
FOR THE SCHOOL YEAR

1. Use a folder or loose-leaf notebook to organize the following information about your child:
- Report cards
- Samples of schoolwork
- Notes from the teacher
- Notes from phone conversations
- Test scores
- Conference notes
- Copies of academic standards for the grade
- School newsletters

2. Create a school calendar (or insert a calendar the school sends home) and include the following:
- School meetings
- School holidays and in-service days
- Important academic events
- School social events

3. Check on your child's classwork and homework throughout the school year. Ask your child questions about his homework and have him explain his answers.

4. Communicate with teachers about your child's progress throughout the school year. Don't be shy! You are your child's best advocate.

5. Note the school web sites and phone numbers you'll need. Write down the username and password you'll use to check your school's online information system for homework assignments, grading databases, and test/transcript info, as well as other systems (lunch accounts and school district information).

TOUCH BASE !

We're looking forward to forming a great partnership with you this year. One of the first steps to becoming an involved parent is telling us how we can best communicate with you. Write your contact information below and let us know what ways work best to get in touch and *stay in touch* with you!

Your Name _____

Your Street Address _____

Your E-mail Address _____

Your Phone Numbers _____

                             [Home]   [Work]   [Cell/Pager]

Your Child's Name, Age, and Grade/Group _____

Your Child's Address and Home Phone [if different from yours]

Special Information We Should Know

HELPING KIDS WITH HOMEWORK

Let your kids know you value the learning that comes from doing homework regularly, completely, and on time. Homework reinforces new concepts, lets your child review the day's work, and gives practice in mastering new concepts and skills.

Help your child be successful and confident with homework by following these tips:

- **Identify an area where your child can do homework.** It can be the kitchen table, a desk or activity table, or even a lapboard and comfy chair. If your child comes to your workplace after school, find a comfortable spot where she can read and work quietly. What matters is that the place becomes associated with doing schoolwork and is a place where your child can concentrate.

- **Give your child a healthy snack (food and drink) after school** before he settles down to study.

- **Allow a reasonable amount of time to exercise or "blow off steam"** before he starts homework. Children arrive home having been "good" for seven or more continuous hours, and need unscheduled time to make a successful transition to home and its demands.

- **Provide your child with the following supplies for completing assignments:** Good lighting (a reading lamp is helpful), lined paper, pencils, pens, an eraser, a folder for each subject, a pencil sharpener, scratch paper for rough drafts and math calculations, a three-ring notebook with dividers for loose papers, spiral bound and composition notebooks (for lab work and school journals), a stapler and staples, a three-hole punch, colored markers and crayons, drawing paper, poster board, transparent tape, glue sticks, scissors, a calculator, a dictionary, a thesaurus (a guide to words that are similar), an encyclopedia (or the school password to access online encyclopedias through the school's media center subscription), a computer, shoeboxes (for school projects and to keep school supplies organized), graph paper (for older students), and a water bottle.

- **An uninterrupted night's sleep (9–10 hours on average) is key for kids' work productivity,** concentration, and understanding of new concepts. Some still need a "rest period" or even a short nap after school before settling into the homework routine. If you can monitor your child's sleep habits and make sure she gets the sleep necessary for high performance, you will be setting her up for success with tasks that require concentration.

- **Serve as a "homework helper" in the early years, gradually easing back as kids approach the middle school grades.** You'll find yourself becoming more a homework advisor and less a homework partner as time goes by. Teachers expect students in middle school and beyond to do most of their homework independently, with only occasional assistance from you.

- **Identify any areas in which your child experiences academic weakness (math? reading? writing? general inattentiveness?) and take action.** Do one or more of the following: make arrangements for your child to meet regularly with the teacher for tutoring during times the teacher specifies; enroll your child in a community-based tutoring program; seek homework help through your after-school or daycare provider; ask for supplemental materials from the teacher; and hire a private tutor.

- **Don't be shy about asking for help from your child's teacher when you are puzzled, confused, or need support.** Use every tool at your disposal to ensure your child's academic success: call your school's homework help line; check teachers' and the school's Web sites and e-mail newsletters; use a computer to connect to the public library and use library homework links; seek out neighbors who have special knowledge of a content area they are willing to share with your child; read books on the subject; and take community education parenting classes.

PARENT HOT MAIL—ASSIGNMENT ALERT!

Teacher, Class, and Contact Information:

The Assignment and Brief Description:

The Final Due Date _____

Steps Along the Way (and intermediate due dates):

For more information and help, where can parents go?

SHARE YOUR PARENTING SKILLS, HOBBIES, AND INTERESTS!

....

Do you have a creative hobby, work-related skill or craft, favorite recipe, language and culture, cherished family tradition, or special experience you'd like to demonstrate?

Please sign up to share your special gift with us. We'd be honored to have you as our guest!

....

Name: _____

Address: _____

E-mail Address _____

Phone Numbers: _____
                        [Home]   [Work]   [Cell/Pager]

Child's name, age, and grade/group:

Your special gift or interest:

Days and times you are available:

Equipment you'll bring with you:

Materials or equipment you need us to provide:

CAR POOL CO-OP

Don't have a car or need help with driving? Want to save fuel, put less wear and tear on your tires, and get a little time to yourself? Then how about sharing the road with other families in your area by joining a car pool?

Sign up below to add your name to a master list of drivers. We'll be in touch!

Driver's Name: _____

Child's Name: _____

When You're Available to Drive: _____

When You Need a Driver: _____

Phone Numbers: _____

              [Home]   [Work]   [Cell/Pager]

Address: _____

E-mail Address: _____

Your Car's Make and Model: _____

Number of Seatbelts: _____

Your Auto Insurance Company: _____

Your Driver's License (State and Number): _____

Special Information:

FAMILY VISIT REMINDER

I'm looking forward to visiting with you and your child very soon! Please look over the following information and keep it with your family calendar. It will be wonderful to get to know you.

Who Will Come:

When We'll Get Together:

Where We'll Meet:

What We'll Talk About:

How to Reach Me:

Please let me know if you need to make any last-minute changes, and I'll gladly reschedule the visit.

Dear Elementary School Parents and Guardians,

Welcome! We are pleased you and your child are a part of our school community this year. With your help, it will be a year of growth, achievement, and success for your child, and a year in which you are involved with and feel supported in your child's learning.

Education experts agree that parent engagement is critical to a young person's successful school experience. Active parent involvement in children's early school education is critical to their academic, social, and healthy emotional growth.

Young children develop rapidly during the elementary years. You will see many changes in your child throughout the year. You can best support your child by offering nutritious meals, enforcing a regular bedtime, and helping organize backpacks and belongings for the next day. Help your child learn the importance of good study habits, read with her or him each day, point out patterns and "how things work" in the world around you, and make time for your child to enjoy caring friendships with other children.

Your child will be excited and proud to see you at school. He or she will benefit from your participation in our school community, so please consider volunteering. Be assured that **students whose parents are involved in their school experience make better transitions** to middle school and, eventually, to high school. **They experience more academic success and make more positive behavior choices.**

We want to support you in your efforts to be involved in your child's education at our school. Parent involvement is much more than volunteering—it is a productive collaboration between parents and staff to give children a foundation of structure, support, and realistic expectations for their learning and achievement.

We have put together practical ideas for different kinds of parent involvement based on education research. We hope you'll take these suggestions to become a happy, effective partner with your child's school community.

Thank you for becoming involved!

Principal _____

Parent Involvement Coordinator _____

Dear Middle School Parents and Guardians,

Welcome! We are pleased you and your child are a part of our school community this year. With your help, it will be a year of growth, achievement, and success for your child, and a year of continued involvement and support for you.

Education experts agree that parent engagement is critical to a young person's successful school experience. Parent involvement in children's school lives often takes a different form once children reach middle school because of the unique developmental characteristics of the young adolescent. Children in the middle grades are becoming more independent, academically, socially, emotionally, and physically. While their bodies more closely resemble those of young adults, they still have many needs that only you as a parent can meet. They need you in important ways to help ease the many transitions they are experiencing.

Your child might voice concerns about seeing you at school (or about having her or his friends see you). Even though your child may no longer hug you in the hallway, he or she will benefit from your participation in our school community. Be assured that **students whose parents remain involved make better transitions** to middle school and, eventually, to high school. **They experience more academic success and make more positive behavior choices.**

We want to support you in your efforts to be involved in your child's education at our middle school. Parent involvement is much more than volunteering—it is a productive collaboration between parents and staff to give children a foundation of structure, support, and realistic expectations for their learning and achievement.

We have put together practical ideas for different kinds of parent involvement based on education research. We hope you'll take these suggestions to become a happy, effective partner with your child's school community.

Thank you for becoming involved!

Principal _____

Parent Involvement Coordinator _____

Dear High School Parents and Guardians,

Welcome! We are pleased you and your child are a part of our school community this year. With your help, it will be another year of growth, achievement, and success for your child, and a year of continued involvement and support for you.

Education experts agree that parent engagement is critical to a young person's successful school experience. Parent involvement in children's school lives often takes a different form once children reach high school because of the unique developmental characteristics of the young adolescent.

High school students are becoming steadily more independent and are learning to make many kinds of personal decisions and behavioral choices. They are beginning to think about their futures and about the kind of people they will become. Your child might voice concerns about seeing you at school (or about having her or his friends see you), but remember that he or she will continue to benefit from your involvement in our school community. **Students whose parents remain involved make better transitions** to postgraduate settings, and **they experience more academic success and make more positive behavior choices.**

We want to support you in your efforts to be involved in your child's education at our school. Parent involvement at the high school level is much more than volunteering—it is a productive collaboration between parents and staff to give children a foundation of structure, support, and realistic expectations for their learning and achievement.

We have put together practical ideas for different kinds of parent involvement based on education research. We hope you'll take these suggestions to become a happy, effective partner with your child's school community.

Thank you for being involved!

Principal _____

Parent Involvement Coordinator _____

MAKING THE MOST OF READING!
CLASSROOM INVOLVEMENT IDEAS FOR PARENTS

Can you see yourself participating in the following activities? These inclusive activities work for all parents, including those whose first language is not English. Check the boxes that interest you, and return this form to your child's teacher.

My Name: _____

My Contact Information: _____

_____

I am interested in helping with the following activities, and I can:

○ Promote Black History Day, the Underground Railroad, and African Odyssey by coming in costume and reading stories on these themes to the class.

○ Organize Read and Recycle Club, which encourages children to bring gently used books to school. Children can bring and exchange their book for another book (or they can bring multiple books, which can be purchased for 25 cents).

○ Organize a book fair with the Parent-Teacher Organization through a recognized book organization. Parents set up book displays, help children find books on the topics of their choice, invite families after school to join in, and repack books at the end of the event.

○ Promote a reading contest in each class (number of minutes spent reading or number of pages read), and hold a book giveaway for classes that reach their goal.

○ Help with a Drop-Everything-And-Read (DEAR) Day. Students bring their pillows and a blanket or sleeping bag and "camp out" in the classroom with a good book and popcorn or a special snack. Parents read to small groups in quiet corners.

○ Accompany students on a trip to a local newspaper office to learn how the news is investigated, reported, and distributed. Help students find their way around a newspaper and identify sections they would like to read.

○ Invite elders and grandparents to join them in the classroom for a special Elder Day. Elders can share with the students the importance of reading through their own favorite children's stories.

○ Be special guest readers who read short stories in their native languages to children. Children can then read the story in English and discuss the similarities and differences in meaning (if any).

○ Create a beach party event in the school gym with special props. Have students come in shorts and T-shirts, and provide sunglasses and beach towels to lounge on as they read comic books and favorite paperbacks.

○ Set up a special theme day: European Cafe, Native American Games, Asian Arts and Activities, African Safari, or Australian Walk-About, and tie in books and readings to the theme. Provide art activity stations and writing- and reading-related games.

CONNECT WITH LANGUAGE TRANSLATORS AND SCHOOL LIAISONS

Do you need help with language translation or school-related questions? For assistance, call or e-mail one of the translators or liaisons below.

Name & Title: _____

Language(s): _____

E-mail: _____

Telephone: _____

Best Times to Call: _____

Name & Title: _____

Language(s): _____

E-mail: _____

Telephone: _____

Best Times to Call: _____

Name & Title: _____

Language(s): _____

E-mail: _____

Telephone: _____

Best Times to Call: _____

HOPES AND DREAMS

Let's start the new year with a look at your parenting hopes and dreams for your children's growth and achievement. What hopes do you have for your child this year? What are your child's hopes? What kinds of support do you need to make those hopes real?

Write your hopes and dreams for your child below. Add any suggestions you have for getting started.

My Child's Name: _____

My Name and Relationship to Child: _____

My Contact Information: _____

_____

My Hopes and Dreams for My Child This Year:

My Child's Hopes and Dreams for This Year:

My Concerns for My Child:

My Child's Concerns:

What I Need from You:

PARENT TIPS: PREPARING CHILDREN FOR A PERFORMANCE

Part of growing up for most children is taking part in public performances. Help kids relax and do their best by preparing them in advance. Try these suggestions for letting kids shine:

Practice Makes It Better!

1. **See and hear the positive parts of your child's efforts.** Reinforce with specific remarks such as, "You project your voice so well that I can hear you in the back of the room."

2. **Don't focus on a mistake.** If you need to, mention it briefly, offer a helpful suggestion, and then move on.

3. **Decide how many times your children will practice a certain part and leave it at that.** This technique helps keep the performance in perspective.

4. **Let your child visualize the performance.** Describe what will happen before the performance, where the audience will sit, where you'll be, and where she or he should go when it's over.

5. **Talk about the clothes your child will wear.** Offer some choice, if possible, and focus on your child's comfort.

6. **Model a low-key attitude.** Don't allow tension to overwhelm your child. Encourage high standards, but don't overemphasize a single performance.

7. **Give your child many opportunities to practice and ask questions.**

On the Big Day

1. **Build extra time into your schedule so that you can address last-minute surprises.**

2. **Make arrangements with drivers and chaperones in advance.** Keep their contact information handy for last minute changes of plan. Have a master list of kids and chaperones with you, as well as a pen and pad of paper.

3. **Help your child review the props, equipment, and clothing she or he needs before the performance begins.** Be prepared to make substitutions.

4. **Address your expectations for your child's behavior in advance.** Explain clearly what is and is not appropriate. Have an exit plan if your child becomes sick.

5. **Offer a healthy snack before the performance, and stick to a regular meal schedule.**

6. **Before the performance, let your child visit the bathroom, take a drink of water, and draw deep, relaxing breaths to clear her or his head.**

7. **Remind your child to have fun and enjoy the performance!**

8. **After the performance, offer complete acceptance of your child's efforts.** Saying "I'm proud of you" is very powerful. Minimize talk about mistakes and focus on the good things. Offer an appropriate treat that's low-key and focused on the group context (for instance, offer cookies to everyone).

A PARENT'S CONFERENCE PLANNER

Date, Time, and Location: _____

Parent Name: _____

Parent Contact Information: _____

Child's Name: _____

As you think about the ways your child learns best, what would you like your child's teachers to know about your child?

1. My child learns best by doing the following:

2. I have the following questions about my child's learning styles and situation:

3. My child is successful when:

Ask your child to help you answer the following questions.

1. What do you like best about school?

2. What do you not like about school?

3. Who are your friends at school?

4. What would you like your teacher to know?

A PARENT'S GUIDE: QUESTIONS TO ASK DURING THE CONFERENCE

Please feel free to ask any of these questions during the conference. You can add others that are important to you.

1. How does my child's work compare to your expectations for grade-level reading, writing, and math?

2. If my child's work is either below or above grade level, what strategies are you using to address his or her level? What strategies do you suggest I use at home?

3. May I please see examples of my child's schoolwork? May I see a sample of grade-level work so that I can make a comparison between the two?

4. Please describe my child's strengths and weaknesses in your class.

5. What are your expectations for academic and behavioral achievement for children in your class?

6. What strategies can I use at home to support my child's schoolwork?

7. What is the best way to communicate with you when I have questions or need help with my child's schoolwork?

GETTING ORGANIZED AFTER THE PARENT-TEACHER CONFERENCE

1. **Talk with your child about how the conference went.** Praise your child's strengths. Mention one or two areas in which your child can improve. End with a compliment to your child.

2. **Decide together how you want to carry out any plan that you and your child have agreed upon with the teacher.**

3. **Fill a folder or loose-leaf notebook with the following information about your child:**
   - Report cards
   - Samples of schoolwork
   - Notes from the teacher
   - Notes from phone conversations
   - Test scores
   - Conference notes
   - Copies of academic standards for the grade
   - School newsletters

4. **Create a school calendar (or insert a calendar the school sends home) and include the following:**
   - School meetings
   - School holidays and in-service days
   - Important academic events
   - School social events

5. **Check on your child's classwork and homework throughout elementary school.** Ask your child questions and have your child explain her or his reasoning. Continue to check your child's work periodically throughout middle school.

6. **Continue to communicate with teachers about your child's progress throughout all years of schooling.** Don't be shy! You are your child's best advocate.

7. **Read to or with your child each day through elementary school.** Share your favorite book recommendations and impressions of what you read with your child throughout middle school and high school.

A TOTALLY AWESOME HOMEWORK PLAN !

What is homework time like for your child and you now?

How do you want homework time to be?

Your action plan:

What needs to happen to make this work?

Student: _____

Parent/Guardian: _____

Teacher: _____

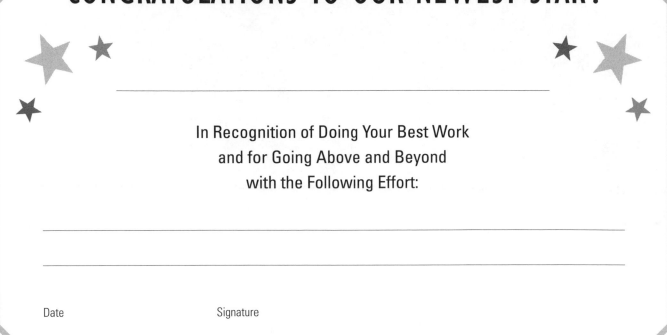

CONGRATULATIONS TO OUR NEWEST STAR!

In Recognition of Doing Your Best Work
and for Going Above and Beyond
with the Following Effort:

Date   Signature

CONGRATULATIONS TO OUR NEWEST STAR!

In Recognition of Doing Your Best Work
and for Going Above and Beyond
with the Following Effort:

Date   Signature

PARENTING BINGO

Has served cereal for dinner.	**FREE**	Knows the names of her/his child's friends.	Has a special ritual with her/his child.	Spends family time outdoors.	Has taken child to a movie or concert she/he disliked, just to spend time together.
FREE	Attends parent-teacher conferences.	Helps her/his child with homework.	**FREE**	Enforces a regular bedtime for her/his child.	Has rules about telling other family members where you are.
Has devoted an entire weekend to a parent-child project.	Considers him- or herself an optimist (why?).	Eats dinner with family most evenings.	Calls home when out of town for work.	Has a regular family meeting at home.	**FREE**
Has thought about her/his child's education beyond high school.	**FREE**	Did or does something to make a school more friendly.	Says "I love you" every day.	Spent yesterday evening at home with family.	Often makes sacrifices in order to attend child's games or concerts.
Knows the school policy on violence/ bullying.	Lets her/his child's friends spend time at her/his home.	**FREE**	Volunteers in a school.	Knows the school's cheer or fight song.	Knows the names of her/his child's teachers.

GRAND PANDEMONIUM!

Get to know your fellow parents, and have fun while doing it. Follow the directions below—do everything listed here and get the signatures to prove it!

Find a person you haven't met before who lives within 10 blocks of you. Have her or him sign here: _____

Find someone who knows how to play a musical instrument. Have her or him sign here: _____

Find someone who does volunteer work in the community. Have her or him tell you about it and sign here: _____

Ask two other people to join you in singing "Row, Row, Row Your Boat" in rounds, and have them sign here: _____

Find someone who has read a book for pleasure in the past year. Ask what the title was, and have her or him sign here: _____

Find someone who is an active participant in a faith community. Have her or him sign here: _____

Do your best impression of a chicken for someone. Have her or him sign here: _____

Find someone who has a friend who is older or younger by at least 20 years. Have her or him sign here: _____

Find someone who had a significant person in her or his past who provided the love and support that he or she needed to get through a difficult time. Have her or him sign here: _____

If you finish filling in all the spaces before time is up, go back to one of the people who signed your sheet and find out more about that person!

SCHOOL VOLUNTEER SIGN-UP

Please return by _____ to _____.

Would you like to . . .
- Be involved in your child's school day?
- Meet other parents?
- Get to know your child's friends?
- Share a skill with your child's class?

We'd love to have you! Please check the volunteer positions you'd be willing to fill. Soon you'll receive a follow-up call or letter with additional information about volunteering. If you have questions about any of the following volunteer opportunities, please feel free to contact me.

My phone number: _____ My e-mail address: _____

Classroom Volunteer
- ○ Parent volunteer coordinator
- ○ Special projects assistant
- ○ Clerical help
- ○ Math and reading tutor
- ○ Class speaker
- ○ Chaperone (field trips and class events)

Music, Arts, and Sports Volunteer
- ○ Sports event chaperone
- ○ Art enrichment volunteer
- ○ Tutor for English Language Learners (ELL)
- ○ Library/media center assistant
- ○ Vocal music program—clerical/accompanist/voice coach
- ○ Band program—clerical/accompanist/instrument coach
- ○ Orchestra program—clerical/accompanist/instrument coach

Schoolwide Volunteer
- ○ Hearing and vision screener
- ○ School directory editor
- ○ Main office (clerical volunteer; telephone support)
- ○ School-awards program
- ○ Before-/after-school program (club leader/activity helper)
- ○ Tutoring program (writing/reading/math)
- ○ School festival/homecoming
- ○ Lunchroom helper
- ○ Special projects fundraising (coordinator/helper)
- ○ Hospitality coordinator (welcome new families; translator)

Other!
○ _____

Your name: _____

Mailing address: _____

E-mail address: _____

Phone: _____

        [Home]   [Work]   [Cell]

Your child's name: _____

Child's grade/teacher(s): _____

Skills, talents, experiences, or interests you'd like to share:

Best time for you: ○ Morning   ○ Afternoon   ○ Evening

VOLUNTEER HERE!

We'd love to have you as one of our volunteers!

Would you like to . . .
- Get involved in your child's [club/team/group]?
- Meet other parents and spend time with friends?
- Get to know your child's friends?
- Share a skill with children?

Please check the volunteer positions you'd be willing to fill. You'll receive a follow-up call or letter confirming your assignment and letting you know what comes next. If you have any questions on what each position entails, please feel free to contact me.

My phone number: _____ My e-mail address: _____

- ○ Parent volunteer coordinator
- ○ Coaching assistant/project assistant
- ○ Clerical help
- ○ Secretary
- ○ Treasurer
- ○ Phone call coordinator
- ○ Newsletter coordinator
- ○ Driver
- ○ Photographer/scrapbooker
- ○ Media/publicity coordinator
- ○ Fundraising coordinator
- ○ Materials and resources coordinator
- ○ Special events chair
- ○ Other _____

Your name: _____

Mailing address: _____

E-mail address: _____

Phone: _____
          [Work]   [Home]   [Cell]

Your child's name(s): _____

Skills, talents, experiences, or interests you'd like to share as a volunteer:

Best time for you: ○ Morning   ○ Afternoon   ○ Evening

VOLUNTEER APPLICATION

Contact Information

Name: _____

Child's Name: _____

Grade and Teacher: _____

Address: _____

City, State, Zip Code: _____

E-mail Address: _____

Phone Numbers: _____
             [Home]   [Work]   [Cell]

Volunteer Information

Volunteer Position:

(1st choice) _____

(2nd choice) _____

Availability: Day(s) _____ Time Range _____

Fluent in the following language(s):

Skill Areas:

Special Interests:

References

Personal Reference (family member): _____

Personal Reference (friend or clergy): _____

Professional Reference (colleague or supervisor): _____

VOLUNTEER SIGN-IN RECORD

Date	Time In	Time Out	Total Time	Name	Phone	Destination

VOLUNTEER NOTEBOOK

Date ———————— Time In ———————— Time Out ————————

Name ————————————————————————————

Address ————————————————————————————

Phone ————————————————————————————

Destination ————————————————————————————

Activity ————————————————————————————

Date ———————— Time In ———————— Time Out ————————

Name ————————————————————————————

Address ————————————————————————————

Phone ————————————————————————————

Destination ————————————————————————————

Activity ————————————————————————————

Date ———————— Time In ———————— Time Out ————————

Name ————————————————————————————

Address ————————————————————————————

Phone ————————————————————————————

Destination ————————————————————————————

Activity ————————————————————————————

Date ———————— Time In ———————— Time Out ————————

Name ————————————————————————————

Address ————————————————————————————

Phone ————————————————————————————

Destination ————————————————————————————

Activity ————————————————————————————

Date ———————— Time In ———————— Time Out ————————

Name ————————————————————————————

Address ————————————————————————————

Phone ————————————————————————————

Destination ————————————————————————————

Activity ————————————————————————————

Date ———————— Time In ———————— Time Out ————————

Name ————————————————————————————

Address ————————————————————————————

Phone ————————————————————————————

Destination ————————————————————————————

Activity ————————————————————————————

THE PARENTS' GOOD SPORT CODE OF CONDUCT

Keep the cheering positive.

Respect the opposing team and fans.

Learn and understand the rules of the game.

Respect the judgment of the officials (even if you disagree with them).

Accept winning and losing with dignity.

Congratulate your child for a job well done, no matter what the game's outcome.

THE PARENTS' GOOD SPORT CODE OF CONDUCT

Keep the cheering positive.

Respect the opposing team and fans.

Learn and understand the rules of the game.

Respect the judgment of the officials (even if you disagree with them).

Accept winning and losing with dignity.

Congratulate your child for a job well done, no matter what the game's outcome.

SUCCESS TIPS FOR CLASSROOM PRESENTERS

You may be used to speaking in front of groups of children, and that's great! Even if you're not, you can be effective and even fascinating in the classroom if you take a moment to remember these key ideas.

1. **Do your homework and ask questions!** Call or e-mail the teacher or leader five to seven days in advance to make sure you understand what's expected. Find out what time you need to be there and how much time you'll have, what resources you can use—easel, chalkboard, overhead projector—and if there are any special considerations you need to be aware of.

2. **Wear a name tag.** Name tags help kids remember your name. If your school or program doesn't provide name tags for volunteers at check-in, make your own and bring it with you.

3. **Be natural and be yourself!** Speak to the kids in a conversational tone, loud enough so that they can hear, and slowly enough so that they catch your words. Use humor, smile, and enjoy yourself.

4. **Kids love props!** Children learn best when they can involve all their senses, and if you have props to pass around, then so much the better. Large maps, framed photos, good-quality slides on a large screen, and three-dimensional models are all terrific for getting your point across. Kids will have a much easier time relating your words and descriptions to a concrete picture, a working model, or a real artifact such as a fossil, a special hat, a piece of fabric, or a recording of music. Bring your props in a battered old suitcase and you'll really grab their attention.

5. **Keep your talk short, simple, and clear.** Use index cards with your main points outlined, but speak in conversational language—don't read it word for word! Tell a story . . . you'll capture their attention from start to finish if you have a beginning, a middle, and an end. If your story involves a child their age, they'll identify even more with your points.

6. **Don't lecture!** Because experiences and vocabulary vary from person to person in the room, don't assume everyone can assimilate detailed data and definitions. Instead, use lots of descriptions and examples, and stop periodically to ask for feedback: Have you ever…? Have you tried…? What would it be like to….? These kinds of questions evaluate kids' understanding. Offer them the chance to ask you questions, too.

7. **Make it into a game.** When they can move their bodies, kids are able to understand concepts on a physical level that they can later remember by reviewing the way the game was played. Work and play can be intertwined this way. If you can use toys, art materials (such as stencils, letter and number forms, play dough, crayons, and lots of scrap paper), and simple athletic items such as jump ropes, balls, and sidewalk chalk, you can help them learn new words and ideas quickly.

8. **Entertain with a well-timed surprise.** Use a trick or surprise at a key point in your presentation and children will remember it. Don't overdo it—a few simple examples will make your point and leave them asking for your return.

9. **Realize that kids see the world from their perspective and limited set of experiences, not from your viewpoint.** Their concerns and opinions will differ from yours. Use their comments as teaching moments, not as times to judge, shame, or put down. Don't be surprised by the occasional personal question they may ask—they are trying to put together a worldview with you in it!

10. **Kids love to move.** You can use movement or improvisation exercises to get your point across, if it's appropriate. It's probably best, though, to use movement at the end of the presentation, as it's hard to settle them down quietly again without first taking a break.

11. **Finally, take it in stride if kids are loud, spontaneous, and even boisterous in your presence.** You are new to them, and therefore exciting. Let them show their interest, but remind them of the need to listen so that you can share all that you are here to share!

SAMPLE FUNDRAISING LETTER

Dear _____,

During the months of April and May, children at _____ School are participating in a "Trek Across America," a health and fitness initiative developed by our school nurse with grant money from the Wellness Foundation.

Students earn "miles" for every 2,000 steps they take on their pedometers, as well as for their fitness activities outside school and for their healthy eating habits. The goal is to complete the 172-mile journey by May 26.

We would appreciate any donations you could give us in the form of a company gift certificate, cash, or small prizes that would reward children who participate in the "Trek." In the past, your company has been very generous with its donations to community groups for worthy causes. We are appreciative of any help you can give us to make our project a success.

Please call me at _____ or our school nurse, _____, at _____ if you have any questions. Thank you for your support!

Sincerely,

Parent Volunteer Coordinator

SAMPLE FUNDRAISING THANK-YOU LETTER

Dear _____,

The children at our school have concluded their successful "Trek Across America," a spring health and fitness walking campaign that encouraged them to take 10,000 steps toward better fitness at school and at home. We are so thankful for your support in the form of _____, which our school nurse used for small prizes given to each child who participated in the Trek.

It is businesspeople and individuals like you who help make our community a nurturing and welcoming environment for all children. Thank you again for your generosity and support!

Best regards,

Parent Volunteer Coordinator

WRITING YOUR LEGISLATORS: ADVOCACY TIPS FOR PARENTS

One of the ways parents can take the lead in decision-making roles that affect children's education is to get involved in policy advocacy. Writing and communicating with elected representatives has a real impact on the direction of representatives' work.

Identify yourself as a constituent and a resident of the person's district. Always include your address and other contact information.

Write in a polite, courteous manner. Thank the elected official for her or his support at the end of your letter.

Whenever possible, use personal examples and stories of how a particular teacher, staff member, or program has directly helped your child.

Use personal examples and stories of how changes to a particular program or to the positions of particular teachers or staff members could affect (or has affected) your child.

Choose one or two points that are most important to you. Expand on them with factual information.

Advocate strongly for your position. For example, if you are asking representatives to vote for an inflationary increase in public funding for all sources of education revenue, then mention that your school district's true financial costs are tied to inflation, just as your own personal costs for food, shelter, and fuel are: 3.2% or higher, annually. An inflationary (cost-of-living) increase allows schools to maintain their current programs and services.

Argue that local school boards need to be given control of their financial resources in order to deliver the best possible education for all their students.

Ask school board members, state legislators, U.S. senators, and U.S. representatives to require that state and federal governments pay for all legislated mandates (federal education laws) that local school districts are required to comply with, including the federal No Child Left Behind Act (NCLB) and the Individuals with Disabilities Education Improvement Act (IDEA).

[Insert your own district's local legislative platform priorities.]

SAMPLE LEGISLATIVE ACTION LETTERS

Use these sample letters to guide you in writing your own powerful calls to action to your elected officials. To make the best impression, put your concerns into your own words when you write your letter. Please review "Writing Your Legislators: Advocacy Tips for Parents." Thank you for taking time to advocate for our children!

Sample Letter 1

[Date]

Dear Senator/Representative/Director _____,

As a constituent, I am writing to let you know that I wholeheartedly support increased funding for our public schools. I am a *[parent/guardian]* with child*[ren]* in the *[school district]*, and I am concerned about budget cuts to *[name a program or feature, such as reasonable past class sizes, the school aide program, or the music/art/tutoring programs; tell your story of how a particular cut has affected your child].*

The quality of life in *[state name]* is based directly on our educated citizenry. If we lose this asset, our state may lose businesses, residents, and its reputation. It is vital that we invest now in our children's education to secure our future.

Please support at least a *[%]* annual inflationary increase to all funding sources necessary for public education. Please allow our school boards the ability to maintain the quality programs our children deserve. Please allow my child(ren) to experience an education that will prepare them to face the challenges that lie ahead, and allow our schools to provide the education that will enable all children to deal with the real challenges of the future.

Thank you for taking the time to read this letter, and for your support.

Yours truly,

[Your Name and Address]

Sample Letter 2

[Date]

Dear Senator/Representative _____,

As you know, public education is a top legislative priority among your constituents, of which I am one. I have a child*[ren]* in *[grade]* in the *[school district]*. I am concerned about the *[dollars]* in budget reductions my district has absorbed. My children have benefited from *[name a program or feature, such as reasonable past class sizes, the school aide program, the music/art/tutoring programs, and describe what you think the result to your child would be to have these programs reduced or removed]*.

Please support a funding increase to statewide public education that reflects today's financial reality: an annual inflationary increase on education revenue that allows *[school district]* to maintain its current high education quality. The funding situation is critical and directly affects that present and future achievement of all our children. Please help stop the erosion of resources to our schools. Thank you for your time and support.

Sincerely,

[Your Name and Address]

VOLUNTEER RECRUITMENT TRACKING

Volunteer's Name: _____

Contact Information:

Conversation Notes:

VOLUNTEER RECRUITMENT TRACKING

Volunteer's Name: _____

Contact Information:

Conversation Notes:

QUESTIONS ABOUT VOCATIONS: TEENS ASK ADULTS

Jobs, Careers, and Life Choices

Use this list of questions to ask adults about their careers, job preparation, and the way their work and home lives fit together.

- What is your present position? How long have you held it?

- What is your family like?

- What do you like most about your job?

- When you were in high school, what careers did you imagine yourself in?
  What were your favorite courses in high school?

- How did your career ideas influence your choice of college or postsecondary school?
  What were you looking for in a college or post–high school program?

- What were your favorite courses in college? What were your favorite activities?

- Did you have a job while you went to school? If so, was it part-time or full-time?

- Did your family have expectations for you? If so, did they influence your career choices?

- How did your personal beliefs influence your studies and career path?

- Did you have any important influences or mentors when you were younger?
  Do you have current mentors and influences?

- Do you run into ethical conflicts at work? How do you resolve them?

- What are your most important accomplishments so far (personal and/or professional)?

- Do you have a philosophy for your work life? If so, will you tell us about it?

- What do you do for fun? How do your hobbies help you do a better job when you *are* at work?

- Is there anything else you'd like to share that will help us think about life after high school?

Thank you so much!

CAREER RESOURCE SPEAKERS

Do you love to talk about your job? If you'd be willing to talk about your profession with kids, sign up below!

Profession: _____

Name: _____

How to Reach Me: _____

_____

Profession: _____

Name: _____

How to Reach Me: _____

_____

Profession: _____

Name: _____

How to Reach Me: _____

_____

Profession: _____

Name: _____

How to Reach Me: _____

_____

Profession: _____

Name: _____

How to Reach Me: _____

_____

Profession: _____

Name: _____

How to Reach Me: _____

_____

Profession: _____

Name: _____

How to Reach Me: _____

_____

Profession: _____

Name: _____

How to Reach Me: _____

_____

PARENT/GUARDIAN
PERMISSION TO PARTICIPATE

The purpose of the activity is:

The activity will take place at the following location:

On (date): _____ at (time): _____

The transportation to be used is:

Children will need the following equipment or clothing:

The following adults will be responsible for your child:

- -

I give my permission for my child to participate in the following activity:

In case of an emergency, I can be reached at (phone number): _____

Signature and contact information: _____

Relationship to child: _____

Date: _____

PARENTS ARE THE BEST!

Thank You
For Making Our School a Better Place!

_____

Name / Volunteer Job / Date

Principal _____   Teacher _____

THANK YOU! GRACIAS! DANKE! MERCI! GRAZIE! OBRIGADO! MIIGWECH! MAHAD SANID! XIE XIE!

We couldn't have done it without you. Your contribution of time, effort, and enthusiasm helped us be successful. Thank you for being a caring, involved parent in our children's lives!

With much appreciation and gratitude,

Additional Information

Online Tip Sheets and Toolkits

The Annie E. Casey Foundation (www.aecf.org) offers many resources for families and communities, including "Strengthening Families/Strengthening Schools Toolkit" report in a downloadable PDF file.

Learning Point Associates (www.learningpt.org) offers tip sheets from the former North Central Regional Educational Laboratory (NCREL) on preparing for and making home visits, creating family and community partnerships, and other pertinent topics, including "Actions Parents Can Take to Help Their Children Succeed in School," "Five Guiding Principles for Involving Parents in Schools," and "50 Ways Parents Can Help Schools."

National Center for Family and Community Connections with Schools (www.sedl.org/connections) offers research summaries and strategies, NCLB parent involvement guidelines, and useful tools for connecting families, schools, and communities.

National Coalition for Parent Involvement in Education (www.ncpie.org) features an extensive array of parent engagement resources for parents, teachers, youth leaders, and administrators.

National Education Association (www.nea.org) has downloadable tip sheets for parents, including "Getting Involved in Your Child's Education," "Bridging the Great Homework Divide: A Solutions Guide for Parents of Middle School Parents," and minority community outreach materials on preparing students for postgraduate education.

National Parent Teacher Association's "Three for Me" Web site (www.three4me.com) provides many free, useful handouts and resources specifically for increasing parent involvement.

The Parent Institute (www.parent-institute.com/educator/resources) offers free tip sheets and parent engagement articles.

Recruiting New Teachers, Inc., offers "Connect for Success: Building a Teacher, Parent, Teen Alliance—A Toolkit for Middle and High School Teachers" for teachers working in high-poverty middle and high schools. See www.eric.ed.gov.

The Teaching Tolerance Web site of the Southern Poverty Law Center (www.splcenter.org/center/tt) provides a wide array of resources and tip sheets for teachers and parents related to parent involvement in the school and community.

Cross-Cultural Resources

Allen, L. M., Simmons, M. W., and Diggs, G. A. (2007). *Engaging African American Families in Their Children's Education.* Westminster, CO: Colorado Statewide Parent Coalition. Retrieved April 4, 2008, from www.coparentcoalition.org.

Arias, M. B. and Morillo-Campbell, M. (2008). *Promoting ELL Parental Involvement: Challenges in Contested Times.* East Lansing, MI: The Great Lakes Center for Education Research & Practice.

Briggs, S. E. and Garcia, M. M. "Volunteer Opportunities for Non-English Speaking Parents." *Teaching Tolerance,* 33 (Spring 2008). Retrieved April 4, 2008, from www.tolerance.org.

Fadiman, A. (1997, 2001). *The Spirit Catches You and You Fall Down: A Hmong Child, Her American Doctors, and the Collision of Two Cultures.* New York: Farrar, Straus, and Giroux.

Garcia, M. M. (2008) *The ABCs of Family Engagement.* Montgomery, AL: Southern Poverty Law Center. Retrieved April 4, 2008, from www.tolerance.org.

Gorski, P. C. "The Question of Class." *Teaching Tolerance,* 31 (Spring 2007). Retrieved April 4, 2008, from www.tolerance.org.

Lucero, M. G. (2000). *The Spirit of Culture: Applying Cultural Competency to Strength-Based Youth Development.* Denver, CO: Assets for Colorado Youth.

Noguera, P. and Wing, J. Y. (2006). *Unfinished Business: Closing the Racial Achievement Gap in Our Schools.* San Francisco: Jossey-Bass.

Paley, V. G. (2000). *White Teacher.* Cambridge, MA: Harvard University Press.

Pipher, M. (2002). *The Middle of Everywhere: The World's Refugees Come to Our Town.* New York: Harcourt, Inc.

Roybal, P. and Garcia, D. T. (2004) *Engaging Mexican Immigrant Parents in Their Children's Education: A Guide for Teachers.* Westminster, CO: Colorado Statewide Parent Coalition. Retrieved April 3, 2008, from www.coparentcoalition.org.

Tinkler, B. (2002). *A Review of Literature on Hispanic/Latino Parent Involvement in K–12 Education.* Denver, CO: University of Denver. Retrieved April 3, 2008, from www.eric.ed.gov.

Wheeler, J. "Opening Doors on the Border." *Teaching Tolerance, 33* (Spring 2008). Retrieved April 4, 2008, from www.tolerance.org.

Research Articles and Policy Briefs

Commissioner's Parents Advisory Council (2007, June). *The Missing Piece of the Proficiency Puzzle: Recommendations for Involving Families and Community in Improving Student Achievement.* Frankfort, KY: Kentucky Department of Education. Retrieved April 3, 2008, from www.kde.state.ky.us.

Cotton, K. and Wikelund, K. R. (1989). *Parent Involvement in Education,* School Improvement Research Series Close-Up #6. Portland, OR: Northwest Regional Educational Lab. Retrieved April 3, 2008, from www.nwrel.org.

Family Strengthening Policy Center (2004, October). *Connecting Families, Schools and Community Resources,* Policy Brief No. 2. Washington, DC: National Human Services Assembly. Retrieved April 3, 2008, from www.nassembly.org.

Family Strengthening Policy Center (2004, October). *Parental Involvement in Education,* Policy Brief No. 3. Washington, DC: National Human Services Assembly. Retrieved April 3, 2008, from www. nassembly.org.

Henderson, A. and Mapp, K. (2002). *A New Wave of Evidence: The Impact of School, Family, and Community Connections on Student Achievement.* Austin, TX: National Center for Family and Community Connections with Schools/Southwest Educational Development Laboratory. Retrieved April 3, 2008, from www.sedl.org.

Horowitz, A. and Bronte-Tinkew, J. (2007, June). *Building, Engaging and Supporting Family and Parental Involvement in Out-of-School Time Programs,* Research to Results Brief. Washington, DC: Child Trends. Retrieved April 3, 2008, from www.childtrends.org.

Redding, S., Langdon, J., Meyer, J., and Sheley, P. (2004). *The Effects of Comprehensive Parent Engagement on Student Learning Outcomes.* Lincoln, IL: Academic Development Institute. Retrieved April 3, 2008, from www.gse.harvard.edu.

What Research Says about Parent Involvement in Children's Education (2002). Lansing, MI: Michigan Department of Education. Retrieved April 7, 2008, from www.michigan.gov.

Acknowledgments

Thank you, first and foremost, to my parents, David and Lucille Tellett, who chaired the PTA at my elementary school, provided cookies for classroom parties (and cleaned up afterward), made costumes and props for youth theater productions at church, reinforced homework time, drove me to after-school activities, and helped in countless other ways. They taught me by example that engaged parents make a difference.

Jumping ahead several decades to the year my first child entered kindergarten, I extend a special thanks to Frank Johnson, principal at Peter Hobart Elementary School in St. Louis Park, Minnesota, who believed that parent engagement mattered, and to the wonderful teachers on his staff, who welcomed parents into their classrooms, knowing that our efforts would make a difference in the lives of the children they were teaching.

Thanks, too, to all the engaged parents who preceded me and worked alongside me, teaching me and other parents what we needed to know about fundraisers, running meetings, organizing events, recruiting other parents, locating and bringing in guest artists, gathering parents to speak at school board meetings, and all the myriad actions we can take as parents to support our children and their teachers.

Through my work at Search Institute, I have met involved parents all over the country, and have heard the stories of school teachers, Little League coaches, Sunday school teachers, after-school program staffers, community initiative coordinators, and many others who bring their creativity and talents to the task of recruiting and engaging parents in the activities that make a difference in their children's lives. Thanks to all of you.

In particular, I would like to thank Linda Silvius of San Jose, California; Ann Thomas of St. Louis Park, Minnesota; Patsy Roybal of Denver, Colorado, and Betsy Fox of Boulder, Colorado. Each one is passionate about building Developmental Assets for and with young people. They have created powerful and effective ways of engaging parents, especially in school settings, and have shared their ideas through interviews and conference sessions so that others can learn from their experiences.

And finally, thanks to Susan Wootten, an editor here at Search Institute who first suggested this project and soon joined me as co-author. Her own experiences have added immensely to the final product.

Nancy Tellett-Royce

It's been my pleasure to join Nancy Tellett-Royce in bringing this book to press. I am thankful to Nancy for her insight, wisdom, and support. I am also privileged to work closely each day with Alison Dotson, whose skills are evident throughout these pages, and with my gifted colleagues in Publishing, Mary Ellen Buscher, Tenessa Gemelke, and Kate Brielmaier. To all my colleagues at Search Institute I say *thank you* for your commitment to positive youth development and for creating an atmosphere of optimism and empowerment that makes this work possible. Finally, to my loving family—Michael, Beth, Molly, and Ben—I offer my gratitude for the many opportunities you've given me to be an engaged and enlightened parent!

Susan Wootten

Index

About the Authors

Nancy Tellett-Royce is a senior consultant at Search Institute, where she has worked for 10 years. She has provided assistance to many of the nearly 600 communities around the United States and Canada that are a part of Search Institute's Healthy Communities • Healthy Youth (HC • HY) national initiative. She has co-chaired and is currently on the executive committee of Children First in St. Louis Park, Minnesota, which was founded in 1992 as the first HC • HY initiative. Nancy and her husband have two sons who have finished high school, and she is a friend and special adult in the lives of many teenagers. She frequently speaks to groups of parents about the power of Developmental Assets.

Susan Wootten is an editor at Search Institute. She taught English and mathematics in Tennessee and North Carolina, and was a freelance editor for 10 years while her three children were young. She has been an active parent leader in school, community, and church-based activities, and currently chairs a parent/teacher curriculum advisory committee in Hopkins, Minnesota.

more great books

CONNECTING IN YOUR CLASSROOM
18 Teachers Tell How They Foster the Relationships That Lead to Student Success

by Neal Starkman

In *Connecting In Your Classroom,* both the humanity and professional secrets of "gold star" K–12 teachers are revealed. The principles of TEACH—trust, engagement, asset building, care, and hard work—are the basis of this inspirational guide to improving teacher-student relationships. Eighteen teachers from across the country share their secrets of how to encourage responsibility, empathy, and hard work—qualities that lead to academic and personal achievement—in their everyday interactions with students. Rooted in the Developmental Assets approach, these narratives inspire concrete, commonsensical, and positive experiences and qualities essential to raising successful young people.

$12.95; 144 pages; softcover, 7"×9"

GREAT PLACES TO LEARN
Creating Asset-Building Schools That Help Students Succeed, Second Edition

by Neal Starkman, Peter C. Scales, and Clay Roberts

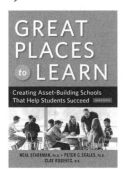

This foundational book is a powerful, positive guide to infusing Developmental Assets into any school community. From building awareness to sustaining system-wide changes, *Great Places to Learn* offers a step-by-step outline to guide school administrators, principals, and teachers through the process of integrating assets into their school while firsthand accounts provide the creative inspiration to adapt the concept to any situation.

Includes a CD-ROM with reproducible handouts, charts, action lists, and assessment tools for everyone—from principals to bus drivers; Search Institute's latest survey data; and discussions on bullying, school vio-

lence, and the effect of the No Child Left Behind Act on school communities.

$34.95; 216 pages; softcover (includes CD-ROM); 7"×10"

GREAT PRESCHOOLS
Building Developmental Assets in Early Childhood

by Tamara J. Will, Karen King and Michelle Mergler

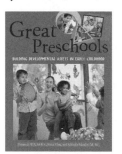

Implementing Search Institute's 40 Developmental Assets for Early Childhood, the content draws from literature and research across the field of preschool development. Eight helpful asset categories provide straightforward and clear direction for educators in both formal and informal preschool settings. Reproducible handouts make it easy for educators to communicate with parents and add fresh ideas and content to any preschool curriculum. Many age-appropriate activities and suggestions for adaptations to group sizes offer new interpretations of familiar songs, books, games, and art projects. Includes CD-ROM with reproducible handouts.

$39.95; 264 pages; softcover (includes CD-ROM); 8½"×11"

HOW WAS *YOUR* DAY AT SCHOOL?
Improving Dialogue about Teacher Job Satisfaction

by Nathan Eklund
Coming Fall 2008!

Founded on the strength-based approach of Developmental Assets, this book advocates collegiality and strong relationships between teachers and administrators—a refreshing alternative to the adversarial roles these two groups often play. Discussion questions and handouts facilitate both personal reflection and institutional problem solving, helping readers identify multiple levels of accountability and change. When every stakeholder in the school environment is empowered to take action, teacher job satisfaction becomes a win-win situation, resulting in a supportive workplace climate that sustains educators in their pursuit of higher student achievement. The accompanying CD-ROM includes reproducible forms and other tools for making these efforts.

$34.95; 128 pages; softcover (includes CD-ROM); 7"×10"

PASS IT ON AT SCHOOL!

Activity Handouts for Creating Caring Schools

Schools where students feel valued, supported, and cared for are the best places to learn. This activity-based resource equips everyone in the school community— teachers, students, administrators, cafeteria workers, parents, custodial staff, coaches, bus drivers, and others—with ready-to-use tip sheets and handouts to create change for the better by building Developmental Assets. The handouts are grouped by locations for asset building—in the classroom, cafeteria, locker room, nurse's office, in meetings, and more! It includes adaptable asset-building tips and ideas, engaging activities, and ideas for integrating Developmental Assets into your everyday efforts.

$24.95; 208 pages; softcover; 8½"×11"

POWERFUL TEACHING

Developmental Assets in Curriculum and Instruction

edited by Judy Taccogna

Powerful Teaching deals with the core of everyday classroom teaching and learning, and shows education professionals how to infuse Developmental Assets into existing curriculum and instruction without starting a new program. The book highlights research-based instructional strategies that teachers can use and adapt to their particular needs, plus real examples in Language Arts, Social Studies, Mathematics, Science, Health Education, and Visual Arts. *Powerful Teaching* allows teachers to focus on individual needs and foster the academic, social, and emotional growth of the whole student.

$42.95; 304 pages; softcover; 8½"×11"

A QUICK-START GUIDE TO BUILDING ASSETS IN YOUR SCHOOL

Moving from Incidental to Intentional

by Deborah Davis and Lisa Race

On top of budget cuts, changing curricula requirements, and dwindling instructional time, teachers and educational assistants are expected to "do more with less." *A Quick-Start Guide to Building Assets in Your School* helps education professionals do just that: make a more positive impact on students with less effort. Teachers can scan each segment separately for dozens of asset-building ideas to incorporate into their next group session. Each section offers reflection questions for teachers ("When do you remember having a voice in your own educational experience?"), as well as school-wide strategies to involve parents, students, and other school staff in creating healthy, caring classrooms.

$9.95; 28 pages; saddlestitched; 8½"×11"

SAFE PLACES TO LEARN

21 Lessons to Help Students Promote a Caring School Climate

by Paul Sulley

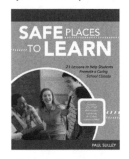

The lessons in *Safe Places to Learn* challenge students to make their school a place where all students feel supported, accepted, and focused on classes, friendship, and fun activities. As a result, school becomes a warmer, safer place for all— teachers, staff, and students. *Safe Places to Learn* offers teachers, counselors, and other caring adults 21 lessons that challenge students in grades 6–12 to change attitudes and behaviors that perpetuate meanness. Students learn to promote kindness, respect, and caring while discouraging gossip, teasing, bullying, exclusion, and violence. They'll know how to effectively stop meanness when they see it—and do it in a respectful, caring way toward both the victim and the bully. Includes CD-ROM with reproducible handouts.

$29.95; 140 pages; softcover (includes CD-ROM); 8½"×11"